WWW ʰⁱ ⁿ... ⁓

MW01268013

Looking *for* Love
in all the Wrong Places

One Woman's Testimony

Twana Nuniss
Revised Edition

GOD'S WAY PUBLISHING LLC

Revised Edition 2016

Unless otherwise stated, my scriptural quotations in this volume are from the King James Version of the Bible.

For further information contact:

God's Way Publishing

twananuniss@gmail.com

Design by Borel Graphics

Photography by istockphoto.com

Edited by Stephany Spaulding

Book consulting by Patrick Oliver

Printed in the United States of America

ISBN 13: 978-1-5398-6052-5

19 18 17 16   6 5 4 3 2

Dedication

I dedicate this book to my children, Corey, Tashona, Katecia, Jeremiah, to my grandchildren, Tionna, Jahkori, Zakiyah, Davine', Maj'ae, Malachi, Phylashia and Micah, to my parents, Edward London SR, Ora D. London and Ulysses Griffin, to my grandmother, Mrs. Cora Lee Joyner and (the late) John Arthur Joyner SR, Mrs. Doshia London and (the late) Henry L. London. My siblings, god-children, and the "Joyner Eight" who treated me like their sister instead of niece. I love you all.

In Loving memory of:
My father, Edward L London Sr, (June2013) and my brother Courtney W. London, (September2014) Rest in Love

Thank You

*F*irst, "Thank you Lord"!!! Thanks for the vision that was so large I could not grasp it in the beginning and for the endurance to continue to write when I did not feel like it. Most importantly, thank you for your Son, Jesus who protects me as I travel to my destiny.

To my friend, Solathian, thanks for always being there for me and believing in the "anointing" on my life when no one else did. God has used you over the years to be a blessing to me in so many ways. I thank you for recognizing your Father's voice and obeying. I am grateful for your friendship.

Thanks to my friends, Deborah, Rosalyn and Shirley. You all were the ones in the trenches with me as I wrote this book over the years and also the ones who believed in the vision the most.

To Karan, thanks for mentoring and loving me like a true sister. I went through a bumpy transition in the beginning of *my changed life* and you were always there, not babying me, but loving me enough to tell me to "get up!"

Thanks to Pastor Al and Monique Montgomery, for mentoring me for 7 years and for encouraging me to walk according to the call that was on my life. I am truly grateful.

Thanks to Mr. Patrick Oliver, Ms. Stephany Spaulding, and Mrs. Denise Borel Billups, who served as my consultant, editor and graphic designer, respectively. I enjoyed working with each of you and appreciate all of your hard work.

Readers, please note that many of the names have been changed to protect the innocent and not so innocent, God knows the difference.

Contents

~ *Chapter* I ~

~ *Chapter* II ~

Contents

Contents

~ *Chapter* VI ~

~ *Chapter* VII ~

~ *Chapter* VIII ~

Contents

Preface

I have searched for love and failed miserably most times, not realizing that love was not something for which a woman should have to search. Why was I so desperately searching for love you may ask? I wondered the same thing. It was only after doing this self-reflection that I was able to pinpoint events that occurred in my life, some subtle, others not so subtle, that shaped me into the person I was then and am now. One thing these events all had in common was each caused me to seek for acceptance and love without counting up the cost or even realizing that there would be a price to pay spiritually for my actions.

I share my story in hopes that I can help someone reflect and realize that they too have been *looking for love in all the wrong places.* I also aim to provide readers an option that will never leave them nor forsake them and will be with them until the end of time.

Foreword

If you have not yet come to the place where you have to face a difficult place in your past, then just keep on living. I met Twana many years ago, she was at a very difficult place in her life, her marriage was in a shambles, she was not saved, and in a strange country with no family for any sort of support. She gave her life to God and immediately He (God) asked her to begin a relationship with me, a woman who was known as strange, a woman who every time she saw me in church, I was weeping on the floor.

God was calling her to unfamiliar territory, a place where it took faith to walk something she knew nothing about. However going to this place propelled her through a journey that would make her become the woman of God that she is today. She had to over come some issues from the past and she had to come to the realization that she was looking for love in all the wrong places.

I want you (Twana) to know that I truly love you and that I'm so proud of the woman of God that you have become. I want to thank you for sharing your testimonies with the rest of us. I know through your life story, this book will cause others to seek first the love of God, and then all other things will be added unto them. I love you Tee.

Shalom,
The Prophetess

Looking *for* Love
in all the Wrong Places

~Chapter I *~*

Humble Beginnings

I was born February 18, 1964 in a small country community near Dewitt, Arkansas. At the time my mother, Ora, gave birth to me, she was only fifteen years old. A midwife, Mrs. Janie Wilson delivered me – my mother had been staying with her temporarily awaiting my birth. In that era, it was somewhat disgraceful to be unwed and pregnant at such a young age. Thus, it must have been hard for my mother to cope with being pregnant and trying to go to school at the same time. Eventually things became too much for my mom to bear and she dropped out of school never to return. I used to think it was because of me that my mom did not receive her diploma and possibly pursue other things in her life. I even have often wondered if she resented me for it. I can only imagine the obstacles she must have faced and I am almost positive that the pregnancy had a lot to do with some of the issues she dealt with later in her life. My mother and biological father were not together, although he had tried to "do the right thing" by offering to marry her when she became pregnant. My dad, Ulysses, was very handsome and smart, but destiny did not allow the two of them to marry. Whether or not my mom realized it was destiny, I do not know. She had her own reasons for not wanting him to be her husband and declined his offer for marriage. Shortly after my birth, my grandparents took me and placed me in their bed. I slept there until the age of four.

~ · ~

When I was a little over one in age my mother became pregnant again. It was during this time that she also met and fell in love with a man named Edward. On January 20, 1966, she gave birth to my little brother, Keith, just as I was about to turn two. Edward had been drafted into the Army during the Vietnam War and was due to leave within a few months. He asked my mother to marry him and she did. Once he left for Vietnam, my mother, Keith and I continued to live with my grandmother until his return in 1968. After living with my grandmother and Edward's mother for several months, my mother and new stepfather eventually moved into their own place taking Keith with them. I continued to live with my grandmother.

I have heard that my aunts and uncles had me pretty spoiled since I was the youngest in the house. My Uncle Charlie bought me my first pair of shoes and won me a souvenir Coca Cola at the fair, my mom still has that Coke. My Aunt Ada, my biological dad's sister, bought me a bear that I had until the ears fell off and my Aunt Gwen even took me to school with her on her last day of school before summer break one year. They say I clowned. I don't remember that but they claim when she asked me to sit down I told her I would "he-haw" her! What in the world was a he-haw?

I can only imagine that I must have been mimicking what is said when the karate men break boards with their karate chops and yell "heeee-haaaaw", I heard everyone, except my Aunt Gwen, thought my little attitude was cute.

Everything was pretty much going in my favor at my grand-parent's home until one day, when I was between four and five years old, my mother and stepfather came to my grandparent's home and began taking my things out and began putting them into their car. I stood by my grandmother as she sat on the couch crying and watching them carry things out. Her crying made me cry. I didn't know why we were crying, but I had never seen my grandmother cry before, so I knew it must have been terrible. Little did I know that not only were the clothes going, so was I. I remember that feeling just like it was yesterday. I cried all the way to my mom and step-father's place and my mom said I cried myself asleep once I got there. I still had my arms still tightly folded as they had been when my stepfather carried me out of my grandmother's house.

I had been calling my grandmother "momma" for years and to be taken away was very painful. Although we moved only five minutes away, the hurt that my grandmother and I both felt that day is what I feel bonded us for life. Unbeknownst to me, this would only be the beginning of many painful events in my life.

Psalm 73:21 "Thus my heart was grieved,
and I was pricked in my reins."

Wounded for Life?

As time went on I began to adjust to living with my mom and stepfather. I can't really remember a lot about that year between when I moved from my grandmother's and started school but my first years of school were great. I had everything imaginable that a kid could have for school as well as the best clothes. My mom and stepfather took real good care of us and my step-father never made me feel like a step-child. I was his daughter and he made me feel as such. Soon there were three of us when my mom gave birth to my brother Edward Jr., steadily we were becoming more and more like a family. Although I knew my mom was my biological mother, I had grown up with her being more like my sister. I loved her and I knew she loved me, however, although I was young, I still felt out of place or like something was missing. My mom and stepfather were pretty young when they married and were still learning how to be parents. As a child, I did not understand that because my grandmother had nurtured me from birth that I had formed a bond with her that was meant for my biological mother. I did not understand what I felt at that young of an age, but there was a void.

I didn't have a relationship with my biological father because he lived in another state and I would only see him when he occasionally came to Arkansas to visit his mother and other family. I had other brothers and sisters from him, but we did not have a relationship due to the geographical distance between us. When my father would come to Arkansas, he would come and pick me up and I would spend time with my brothers and sisters at his mother's house or one of my other great aunt's homes. My grandmother Sadie and grandfather Ollie were very kind to me. Although I did not spend a lot of time with them, they would often ask about me and when I was around them, they showed me love.

Weekdays with my family were pretty normal, but on weekends when my parents would go out, my brothers and I looked forward to spending time at our Grandmother Cora and Grandfather Arthur's house. I was especially close to my mother's youngest sister, Annette, because we were close in age. She was my hero, for I always thought she was so smart with great imagination to write and share stories with us. The stories she wrote were mainly horror stories that she read before we had to go to bed. I never understood why she liked stories about people getting hurt or killed but they were nevertheless good. Annette probably could have been the female version of Stephen King easily. *Humpty Dumpty Magazine* even wanted to publish one of her short stories—"Beware: Thin Ice." Annette's love for writing inspired me to write and throughout my young years I wrote short stories and poems in hopes of one day being able to write stories like her. I also remember spending time with my other aunts and uncles and watching them come home for lunch in the summers when they would have to work in the cotton fields with my grandfather. They were an interesting bunch and were very close. My grandfather was strict in a kind way and did not like for his children to be at odds with one another. My brother's and I spent many nights with them on weekends.

One particular weekend at my grandmother's I remember more than any other. My brothers and I were at my grandparent's asleep as it was late, when my grandparents and I awakened to a lot of noise in the living room. My stepfather and mom were arguing. They had been out to the club and now my dad for a reason unknown to me was irate with my mother. My grandmother got up and beat my grandfather getting into the room. She was trying to calm my parents down before they woke up everyone else in the house. On my weekend visits to my grandparent's home, I generally slept in the bed with them, thereby being privy to much more that occurred in the house. I remember going into the living room, seeing my parents, and thinking that my dad was going to kill my mother. He wasn't punching her, but there was a lot of yelling and pulling. It was my first time seeing them that way so I was very confused. My grandfather made it into the room and immediately began to get matters under control. My grandfather was a soft spoken man, but yet when he spoke, you knew he meant business.

I got so scared that I just started shaking and ran and jumped back into the bed. It amazes me that when I reflect back, I can still feel how I felt that night and remember the event as if it were yesterday. I have come to realize how impressionable children are and how the things we do in front of them can affect them for the rest of their lives if not corrected. That night has stayed with me all these years. It was the first time I saw my parents fight – it definitely would not be the last.

Psalm 27:10 "When my father and my mother forsake me, then the Lord will take me up."

Pre-Teenage Years

Over the years my mom and step father would often get into arguments and sometimes they even became physical with one another. At the sound of their voices elevating, my heart would immediately start racing with the same fear I felt years before taking over me. Sometimes just my reaction would cause the fight to subside, but other times my mom pushed my dad to a place where things would get physical. I always screamed and my stepfather always tried to comfort me, but the damage had already been done. My mother and step father loved each other and there were more good times than bad times. He was her king and she was his queen. He showered her with gifts and new cars every year. She never really had to work and was mainly a housewife. When there were altercations, my brothers were mainly quiet during the occurrences. I think that they knew big sister was there and would somehow try to intervene. Though the bad times were far and in between, whenever I would hear their voices elevating, I would automatically get nervous and cry.

Although I had much of the material things I needed and desired as a child, I was lonely most times and spent my days pretending or writing. Living in a rural area there wasn't much to do, so I spent most of my time playing make-believe. During this phase in my life I also did not like how I looked, therefore, growing up I had low self-esteem. All the things that are socially praised now were not in style then. If you did not have light skin you were not considered beautiful. My mom is a pretty dark caramel and my dad is very light. I remember my mom telling me how my biological father thought I was not his initially because I was dark-skinned and neither of them was. I've often joked about how God must have looked at me and said, "Now she is already going to be something else, so we can't give her light skin and green eyes like her daddy!"

It was only after the addition of the fourth member of our family, my sister, Shenice, that all of the physical altercations between my mom and step-father stopped. I was in the fifth grade at this time. Shenice was his first biological daughter and he spoiled her rotten. She is without a question a daddy's girl. I don't know if my parents had just matured or if they just did not want another one of their daughters' to be affected by their physical altercations. Whatever the reason, I was just glad that it stopped. I loved my step-father to death. The only reason I am even referring to him as my step-father is so you will know who I am talking about. Although the things I witnessed between he and my mother scarred me, I never stopped loving him because I knew he loved me as much as he knew how and never meant to hurt me. However, somehow, in the midst of it all, that void I had inside of me had gotten larger and my search for love began.

Song of Solomon 8:7 "Many waters cannot quench love, neither can the floods drown it: If a man would give all the substance of his house for love, it would utterly be contemned."

Puppy Love

By the time I made it to sixth grade I was a big time tomboy. I loved playing basketball on the pee-wee team at school, riding bikes and hanging out with my brothers. It was during this time that I began developing as a woman, but had not begun my menstrual cycle. Guys liked me, but because I really was not into romantically liking boys it would make me angry when they would stare at me or write those notes asking "do you like me" "circle yes or no." I always circled "no!" There was one guy in particular who would put letters in my locker, which made me really angry so I confronted him at lunch one day and I never had that problem again. I don't remember where I got the little brown puppy that I affectionately called "puddles" but somehow he came into my life. I loved him so much. Although I was not allowed to keep him in the house, I would bring him in sometimes and it seemed as soon as he would come inside, he would urinate on the floor leaving small "puddles" which is how he acquired his name. Although it may seem silly, Puddles had become my confidante. I shared my secrets and dreams with him, sure that he would not breathe a word. One day I came home from school and puddles did not greet me as normal. When I entered the house, my mom broke the news to me that puddles had been hit by a car earlier that day. My brothers buried puddles because I was too busy crying. They did not laugh at me because they knew they would have gotten beaten, so they looked on as I said my last good-byes to my friend. Now who would I talk to?

Also during this time in my life, I began to like hanging out at my grandmother's house even more because I now was old enough to get into my aunts' business. Saturday mornings were spent sitting in the kitchen watching my grandmother press my aunts' hair and them practicing slow dancing with me standing on their feet as if I were their partner. There were lots of laughs and good times. My Aunt Annette, whom I was closest to during this period, was still writing stories and I was still reading them. I was still enjoying school and was still making the honor roll, which always meant my grandmother would bake me something.

Being the oldest and the only girl for a long time of the grand-children on my mother's side meant I didn't have other female cousins my age to play with or share secrets. Now that Puddles was gone, I did not have him either. I did have friends at school and one best friend, Deborah, with whom I shared my secrets. We had been friends since first grade and I enjoyed talking to her but we did not live close enough to each other to hang out other than at school. I also absolutely loved watching afterschool specials. They would come on maybe once a month and I would pretend that I was the teenager in the show. I liked to pretend that I lived in a big city and was able to do the things I saw the kids in the specials doing, like going to the movies with their friends, or a museum, or out with friends to the park. Where we lived in the country, those things were not accessible, therefore I dreamed of the day I would be old enough to move to a large city and experience a different life.

Puppy Love

Out of nowhere it seems, in sixth grade, I began noticing this guy who rode my bus to school. I noticed him constantly watching me and I thought he was so handsome but knew he could not possibly be interested in me. I was just a kid and this guy was much older. Slowly, however, he began to show interest in me. Naturally I was flattered about the fact that an older guy liked me. Before long he began to say little things to me like "you look cute today" or "hey pretty girl." I would cheese showing all of my pearly whites. Riding that school bus those two times a day was the highlight of my life! I didn't care if the bus went to the moon to pick up kids as long as I could look at him each day. What really surprised me was the day he handed me a note as he was getting off the bus. It was the beginning of my first official "puppy love." This guy would write me letters and lyrics to songs, poems, and the whole nine. After months of doing so, he eventually began to tell me how he loved me in his letters. He had become my world. Things at home were okay but my mom had begun working outside the home more and I was often at home with my brothers and sister. Since my mom was out of the house more, our relationship seemed to become more strained. It seemed like I was always getting in trouble for something I did or did not do at the house. Being the oldest came with the responsibility of making sure everything was maintained the way my mother liked it when she and my stepfather were away from the house. This was not always easy with younger siblings running around. By this time not only was my body changing and hormones beginning to rage but I started to seek out ways to get the same type of love and attention that my grandmother had given me in my parent's home. My mother was still a young woman, she was around twenty-seven years old at this time, married and the mother of 4 children. I was seeking for her love and acceptance and I am sure she was still seeking for those very same things. What I felt I was not receiving at home was replaced by my new "crush."

This guy and I would sit together some days on the bus and every day we exchanged letters. It was the highlight of my day. In the letters he began to tell me how he wished I was older so he could take me out on a date. He continued to tell me of how beautiful I was. Although I was in middle school, the high school was right across the street so we would watch the high school students go to lunch while we were still on lunch. This guy was a senior in high school and I was only in 6th grade. The only persons besides the two of us who knew about us was my best friend, Deborah, and his friend Kevin who usually delivered the letters when he wasn't able to do so himself. Every day there was a letter for me. I'm not sure when he began to discuss sex in his letters, but I was a virgin and afraid of having sex. My mom and I had not had a sex talk yet, but I did know where babies came from and how they got there. I heard rumors that he had a girlfriend, one that was his age, but I had fallen in love and did not care. I had already begun to compromise my self- worth.

Proverbs 22:15 "Foolishness is bound in
the heart of a Child..."

A Lesson Learned

Often on weekends when our parents went out, my siblings and I went out also. This was a small town and there were a lot of juke joints – teenagers had their spots and adults had theirs. He and I had been secretly making plans to get together, not even my best friend knew about it because he had sworn me to secrecy. Being so naïve and sprung I was more than willing. One weekend, my parents were planning to go out and I convinced them to let me and my brothers go too. It would probably be the first weekend he and I would be out at the same time. On that particular night, Deborah was not out so I walked around with my Aunt Annette and one of her friends until I saw him and he saw me. Kevin is the one who arranged the hook up. The streets were crowded that night.

My aunt and I were just sitting around talking with some others when Kevin came over and very slickly gave me the look he always gave when he had a letter to deliver so I knew it meant my crush wanted to see me. I managed to steal away from my aunt. Weeks prior I had been practicing kissing on my wrist. I had never kissed a boy before and I was nervous about the whole thing. However, once the set up took place, he made me feel comfortable as he drove to a dark road outside of town. We were in his car and I remember feeling especially nervous because I knew he would

13

probably want to have sex. At this point I was not on birth control and had not even started my menstrual cycle. We began kissing and one thing led to another.

The next thing I know we were in the backseat of his car. I gave away something as precious as my virginity in the backseat of a car and the worst thing of all was that afterwards he looked at me and said, "This wasn't your first time was it?" Though I told him it was he did not believe me. I'll never forget the humiliation that I felt. Just as quickly as I had fallen in love, in that moment I had fallen out. Seven words changed my life and my ideas about love. I realized that he had only been lying to me, for all he had wanted was sex. It wasn't about the song lyrics, and it wasn't about the sweet letters – it was all about sex. He knew I was a virgin because I had told him previously. Still, he took advantage of me and it hurt me tremendously.

I went home that night, washed up and cried my twelve year old heart out. I felt so ashamed because I knew he would probably tell someone and then everyone would know how he had used me. He wrote me a couple of more letters after that night, yet he never mentioned the night we had been together. Instead, he told me how maybe it would not be a good idea for us to talk any longer because he was afraid someone had or would tell my parents about us liking each other and he felt my step father would shoot him. Although my parents had found out I liked him, they did not know that we had been together in that way. I knew it was just his way of breaking things off with me. Needless to say, our letters got shorter and the love I thought I felt had been left in the backseat of his car that night along with my virginity. We never discussed sex again. We never had sex again and eventually we stopped writing letters.

At twelve years old, I did not know about male egos or soul ties. I did not know that when a man and woman connect sexually, they also connect spiritually, which is why sex should be saved for marriage. I had been used and felt ashamed and embarrassed. I had felt closer to him than I had ever felt to anyone other than my family. I did not realize at that time, not only had I lost my virginity, I had lost a piece of my soul.

Matthew 16:26: "For what is a man profited, if he shall gain the whole world, and lose his own soul?
Or what shall a man give in exchange for his soul?"

The Seed

The experience with my first love left me somewhat shaken and I found it difficult to trust boys from that point. I had experienced my first relationship and it left me feeling confused. A seed had been planted, one that unawares to me was slowly growing. I was even too embarrassed to talk to my best friend about it. I walked around with feelings of guilt and shame as I watched him enjoying his senior year and dating other girls. It was as if the letters and the sex had never taken place. In my heart, I wished it hadn't, for I saw myself as less than a person. I had let myself down and did not know how to express what I was feeling. Regardless, to whom would I express these feelings?

Although I felt miserable, I was not a weak person and over time I somehow bounced back out of my depression. I didn't know then that it was God keeping me strong. My family and I visited churches and even belonged to one, but we were not brought up to have a relationship with God. Attending church on Sunday did not mean we sought God or knew to call on Him in times of sadness and distress. If we had known, I'm sure my entire family would have done many things differently. Even still, I have learned that God is so very involved in our lives. When I did not know He was there, He was right there holding my mind and heart. I was looking for solace in other things, unaware of His unconditional love for me.

Romans 5:8 "But God commendeth his love toward us, in that, while we were yet sinners, Christ died for us."

Summertime

he highlight of each year was neither my birthday nor Christmas, although they were both always pretty nice. The highlight for me was always the 4th of July because all of my cousins and uncles from Kentucky would come to Arkansas and we would have a great time. I mainly looked forward to seeing my cousin Tanya who was a couple years older than me. From the time I was around eleven, I would go to Kentucky with her and my other cousins after their visit and stay the entire summer. Her mom and dad loved children and had a huge house in the west end of town. Their house had a swing on the porch and in the evenings we would sit there laughing, joking, and having fun into the wee hours of the morning. Also, Tanya's family lived around the corner from a store and every Friday her dad would give us an allowance and we would head to that store. In addition, our days consisted of playing basketball in the alley, skating on a vacant lot a couple of houses down, and on Friday nights we would ride to Indiana with my cousin's mom to grocery shop at the discount grocery store. Cousin Gerl would buy lots of groceries and cook a big Sunday dinner.

During the week my cousins and I were pretty much on our own, but Tanya's mom always made sure Cousin Howard, her husband, had lunch and dinner every day. He was a minister and during my younger years of staying with them in the summer, we would have to go to church. Once we were older, my cousins and I would hide out on Sunday mornings.

Cousin Howard loved church and singing. We all had a great respect for him and when we knew he was on the way home, we stopped playing spades or anything we thought was ungodly. He had a great heart and I always felt at home in his house. Tanya's brothers were very talented with playing the drums and guitars, her sister, Gina could sing like an angel. Tanya and her other sister, Karen didn't sing, but I think Karen played the keyboard a little bit. They were a close family and being with them reminded me of the times I spent with my aunts and uncles at my grandparents' home. Tanya was more like me, the black sheep of the family. I don't say that negatively because God finds ways to use those of us who are different. She and I were not musical but we were, let's say, adventurous.

Louisville held a secret that I have never shared, until now. I never thought it had an effect on my life but, I know now how much it did and what happened to me unfortunately happens to little girl's every day. Around when I was thirteen and in Louisville for the summer, an older guy began making sexual advances towards me. He was in no way my peer being around twenty or twenty-one years old at the time. It began with touches and later advanced to kissing. Although I had experienced sex once, I was still quite inexperienced. Sometimes he would just hug me, other times there were kisses on the lips or a touch. He always told me not to tell anyone and to keep our encounters secret.

He didn't make advances every day, but throughout the summer there were times when we were alone when he would make advances toward me and attempts to show me his private parts. One night when I was alone, he came into the room where I was and began touching and kissing. I was afraid we would get caught by my cousins and they would think it was my fault. Nonetheless, he said, "I want to make it where you will be able to have sex with all your boyfriends and it will not hurt." He also began telling me how he cared for me and I started to believe him. Then it happened. It was the most unpleasant feeling that I had ever experienced. It was not at all like my first time and I quickly realized that all men were not created equal. I was in a lot of pain afterwards although it had only lasted a couple of minutes. All he did was penetrate me, but because of his size it took him a while. Later, I understood why "my crush" thought I had had sex before my experience with him. Until this night, I had not really been fully penetrated – my hymen had not been broken until now. Resultantly, the feeling that a woman should have on her wedding night was taken by another young man who also had only wanted an opportunity to take my virginity away. I figured something was wrong with me. I had experienced sex twice and yet I did not feel loved. Thinking sex and love were connected, I did not realize that I was still a child and spiritually unable to handle what was taking place. It was like finding out Santa Clause was not real – finding out the truth about something that you treasure changes your life forever.

Although I had never called it molestation that is exactly what it was. I did not realize that it would be a long while before I would ever experience the real love for which I was desperately seeking.

Galatians 4:3 "Even so we, when we were children, were in bondage under the elements of the world"

Wicked Seeds Sown

I returned to Arkansas a different person. Not in looks, but inwardly I had changed. At thirteen, I was going through puberty and feeling awkward about the changes going on with my body. My menstrual cycle started and I officially had become "a woman." The truth of the matter was I had already become a woman in my flesh, but lacked the spiritual maturity to handle the desires of the flesh. The feelings I had should have been preserved for a mature woman, not a thirteen year old girl who had never even had the "birds and the bees" talk. Birds and bees weren't going to cut it now. I had unknowingly stepped into a place that would bring me much heartbreak throughout my life.

When a farmer plants seeds, he does so in hopes of producing a crop. I know this for a fact because my stepfather worked on a farm for many years. There is a particular time of the year to plant and a time to harvest what is planted. After harvesting season, the ground must be tilled for the next year's planting season. One important factor in farming is not to plant the same crop in one field two years in a row. If one plants beans one year, the next year maybe it is rice that's planted. My father explained that after the rice has been harvested, certain chemicals used for the rice helps to produce a better bean crop the following year and vice versa. Planting the same crop in the same field year after

20

year potentially produces a lot of weeds and a poor crop at harvest time.

Satan operates in much of the same way regarding the planting of seeds. He does not plant the same seed from season to season. He changes things up so that when one comes to expect a certain thing, something different happens. Often we think our situations have changed, when in reality our circumstances have only changed appearance. The appearance of my circumstances had changed, for I knew things that I probably should not have known. Additionally, I had experienced things most girls my age had not. All the while I did not realize that whenever a seed physically and spiritually has been planted, if the seed is not removed and is continually nurtured, whatever has been planted will eventually spring up.

Galatians 6:7 "be not deceived, God is not mocked:
for whatsoever a man soweth, that shall he also reap."

It's Spring

*I*n eighth grade I began dating a guy named John, who was in ninth grade. John would turn out to be my on-again and off-again boyfriend throughout high school. He was cute, smart, and clean cut. Though I liked him, I thought he was kind of boring. He never pressured me for sex though. We wrote each other letters, talked on the phone and were both on the basketball team. Everything was going well for us until I started hanging out more and met a guy named Craig.

Craig was totally opposite from John. He was a "bad boy," chocolate and fine, could sing, could dance, and he knew how to talk the talk with young girls. Craig was from another city but during the summer he would come to Dewitt and stay with his older brother. His brother dated my aunt back in the day so they were all good friends. Craig and I met through my aunt and we began talking on occasion. John and I had broken up the summer after my 8th grade year and before I was to leave for Kentucky. During this time Craig and I became sexually active. He was a couple years older than I was and much more sexually experienced. To my dismay, Craig wasn't exactly the faithful type and I heard that while I was in Kentucky for the remainder of the summer, he talked and had sex with other girls. He always denied it, but even young girls have "women's intuition."

The summer ended and so did my relationship with Craig. School started and John and I began to talk again. I was now a freshman in high school and John was a sophomore. Although we were dating again, things were not the same. His expectations had changed as he began to talk about sex. My parents liked John and so did my brothers. Unawares to everyone, our first sexual encounter was right there in my bedroom where I was allowed to have company on weekends. There were no fireworks or special feelings. There was not anything different than any time before. I still felt empty inside when it was over. Although at this point I had only had sex with three other people, spiritually I was actually sexing whomever they had previously sexed also.

Sex at this point in my young life was not enjoyable for me. I guess a lot of it had to do with my previous experiences. None of the guys I had slept with previously loved me and all of the sexual acts I was involved in had only caused my sexual drive to become perverted. I was simply seeking for another moment, just like an addict. I craved fix after fix, not the sex, just the closeness I felt as I pretended the person lying on top of me really loved me. I did not know that my cravings were the results of "soul ties." It's just like the first hit of the crack pipe or the first snort of cocaine, there is a craving, but the subsequent highs are never the same as the first high. As a result, the craving becomes insatiable.

The magical moment that should have been reserved for my husband was gone, never to return and I was searching for love through sex, though I did not know it. I wanted so desperately for someone to love me, but it appeared that no one did. So I kept searching.

1 Corinthians 6:13 "...Now the body is not for fornication,
but for the Lord, and the Lord for the body."

A Mind is A Terrible Thing to Waste

I don't know all of the ingredients required to make a bomb but mixing sex and drugs is probably a pretty good equivalent. By tenth grade I had begun smoking cigarettes and marijuana. It didn't take much marijuana to get me high, laughing and acting a fool, and it soon became my drug of choice. In our town, we could buy a joint on the street for one dollar, cigarettes for fifty cents, and a beer for a dollar. On a Saturday night, if you had $2.50 you were in for a wild night!! I was usually in for a wild night. I really never liked the taste of beer nor that it kept me going to the bathroom, so I usually used the extra dollar for another joint instead of beer. Without a doubt God looks out for fools and babes because there were many nights I drove home without remembering how I had gotten there. When I was high I was carefree, everything was wonderful and my life was no longer boring. The first weed I ever smoked was nicknamed "red-haired ses." The moment I smoked it, I knew it would not be my last. I wanted to always have access to that feeling.

During the week things at our home were pretty normal. The only highlight would be if I were playing in or attending basketball games. The junior and senior basketball teams were pretty good for our district and basketball was the one thing that united the whites and blacks there. As a community, we were the Wildcats and proud of it. My friend Deborah was still my best female friend and my cousin James was my best male friend. James and I talked every day and he was one of the best basketball players to wear a wildcat jersey. I was the one designated to deliver his letters to whomever he was talking to at the time and he delivered my letters to John. It looked like an assembly line as we changed classes because everyone was passing letters and receiving letters on the way to their next class. Although the school was small, we had a lot of good times. Deborah, her sister Peggy, Gayla, Clara, Tangie, Janelle and I would all gather back at the basketball court on our lunch break each day and watch the fellas play basketball as we caught up on our weekend gossip. On non-game days, my brothers and I would ride the bus home from school and follow a regular routine religiously. Our mother was very particular about keeping the home neat, so we all had chores and knew to have them done before she returned home from work. I never got high at home, my mom was too sharp for that. I reserved that time for the weekends only. I wasn't allowed to go out every weekend but usually every other weekend unless my parents were going out too. It may seem strange for parents and kids to be going out together, but that's how our community rolled.

John and I seldom were out at the same time. He wasn't the "going out" type. He liked coming to visit me which I thought was boring. Because John and I had an on again off again relationship as well as Craig and I, I talked to other guys on occasion. Nothing serious, it was not always sexual although I did sleep with a few guys drunk whom I would not have given the time of day sober. I knew that these guys did not truly care for me. The sad part about it was the fact that I really did not care for them either. When the moment was over, my feelings were over. That is the lethal thing about sex, drugs and alcohol. The drugs and alcohol boosts esteem and the sex tears it down. I cannot recall an occasion of casual sex where I did not get up feeling ashamed and dirty. When the high wore off, I wasn't the same person, I had another soul tie. Additionally, I was disrespecting my body and destroying my soul. I was not being taught about soul ties in the church my family sometimes attended. I surely was not learning it at school. My parents and I didn't discuss sex. Still, I was becoming a young woman in age, yet I was spiritually immature. I did not realize that I would one day have to pay the cost for trying to be the boss.

Proverbs 19:3 "The foolishness of man perverted his way, and his heart fretteth against the Lord."

~*Chapter* II ~

I'm Looking for A New Love

Around 11th grade I got my first little car. I say "little," but it was actually a big car, a dark blue 1960's something Pontiac that I affectionately named Bessie. I loved that car. I drove my brothers and me to school and out on weekends. I remember even pin stripping her – she was all that!!

Eleventh grade year was not as boring as tenth grade ended because we were allowed to start practicing in order to get our basketball team back. During tenth grade I took a wine cooler to an out of town game for myself and most of the other girls to drink. I had taken it from our mini bar at home. I had almost forgotten to get it but one of the girls that had come to my house to get dressed for the out of town game reminded me to put it in my bag as we were heading out of the door. Come to find out, our towel girl, Maureen thought it would be cute to fill the bottle with water and leave it in the dressing room. As the comedian Redd Foxx would say, "You big dummy!" Anyway, we ended up getting suspended from school and losing our eligibility to play for a year. My mom was very disappointed in me and showed me how much by beating my butt. I didn't even like drinking at this point. It was just something silly to do, but I paid the price and so did my friends. Now we had our team back and eventually forgave Maureen. We started our basketball year on a positive note and with something we never had–a female coach.

John and I were still dating on and off as usual but now he had even begun seeing other people during our break ups. When it didn't work out with others, we'd end up dating each other again. I had come to the conclusion that we weren't going to be one of those high school romances that would turn into college sweethearts, then husband and wife. It just wasn't going to happen. He was a good friend though, and we still had love for each other, we weren't enemies at least.

Eleventh grade was also when I became acquainted with Patrick. We knew of one another and had even spoken briefly over the years, but it had never been a sexual relationship. He was a couple years older than I was and his uncle ran one of the little clubs young people frequented on weekends. Patrick was very handsome and had a charm about him that should have made anyone skeptical. In other words, he was a player and knew how to talk little girls out of their clothes. We talked a little bit some weekends but never got serious because it had come to my attention that he had a young son and girlfriend with whom he sometimes stayed. His girlfriend was a very jealous person and didn't play when it came to Patrick. But of course me being me, hardened by the lack of love, became insensitive to the feelings of others in that regard, so I was neither intimidated nor moved by that fact. The seeds that were previously planted were steadily growing.

Psalm 73:22 "So foolish was I, and ignorant:
I was as a beast before thee."

29

The Night It Happened

As my junior year was almost over and Spring break was drawing near, I had made plans to spend the week with my aunt Annette to babysit her kids. On Thursday night of my spring break, I walked up the street to see who was hanging out. There wasn't much going on, so I decided to return to my aunt's and was on my way back when a long green car my aunt had nicknamed, "the army tanker," began to roll slowly beside me. The window was down and I saw the cutest smile on Patrick's face. He asked if I wanted a ride and I declined. He, however, continued to ask me until I finally accepted. We pulled in the driveway of my aunt's apartment complex and he turned off the car. We started talking about everything. I liked him, but I felt a little uncomfortable with him. He wanted to come into my aunt's home, but I would not allow it. Sitting in the car, he began touching me, not forcefully at first, but seductively. One thing led to another and we were now horizontal in his backseat.

Ever since I started menstruating I had been on birth control pills at the urging of my mother who suspected that I was having sex. She did not condone my sexual activities, but thought I would be better safe than sorry. While in the backseat of Patrick's car I remembered that I had not been faithfully taking my birth control pills because they sometimes made me feel sick. Thus, I pushed him off of me and told him I could not have sex because I had not taken my pills. He persisted, telling me I could not get pregnant from having sex the first time after missing a pill. Though I explained that it had been more than one missed pill, he persisted.

Patrick pulled vigorously on my pants until he had them completely down and forced himself on me. I cried the entire time because I did not want to have sex with him and was afraid of getting pregnant. He lied saying he would not go "all the way" but did. After he finished, I continued crying and screaming at him about how much I hated him and hoped I wasn't pregnant because I did not want a baby by him. I got out of the car and went into my aunt's house and tried to wash myself clean. It would be two months before I would speak to Patrick again. When I did, he was not prepared for what I had to say.

Psalm 38:18 "For I will declare mine iniquity,
I will be sorry for my sin"

Oops There It Is!

Spring break in March, no period in April, no period in May, my senior year is coming up!! Summertime is here!!! I'm 17 years old!! This can't be happening to me!!! Not now!!! In nine months I'll be having a baby!!! These are all the thoughts that ran through my mind the spring of my junior year after Patrick forced himself on me. I was supposed to be preparing for the time of life that everyone looked forward to, graduating from high school and becoming an adult. Five years earlier I had had a crush on a guy that was a senior, experienced my first kiss, and my first sexual encounter. Now my sins had caught up with me. It was payday.

I don't recall exactly when my mom found out, of course I didn't just tell her. Each morning I got up in hopes that my "friend" would have arrived. It didn't matter how late she would be, I just wanted her to come. To no avail, she was nowhere in sight. All of a sudden my cycle had become my friend and I wanted to see her desperately. I usually called her "the curse," but now I wanted her friendship. My mom realized that she had not bought me pads in a while and was becoming suspicious. I wasn't as smart as the girls are now. I didn't hide the unused ones to keep my mom buying them while I girdled down and prayed for a miracle. I was so tormented in my mind that I felt like I wanted to die. My world was crashing down around me and the bad part was that my mother was acting strange.

I would often catch her looking at me weird. I wanted to confide in her but was too afraid. I knew she would be disappointed but my greatest fear was that she would kill me. Not physically, but with her words.

One day out of the blue my mom made me get dressed so she could take me to the doctor to confirm her suspicions that I was pregnant. To make matters worse, we picked up my grandmother. My mom began telling my grandmother about how she thought I was pregnant and how "fast" I was. I sat in the backseat crying the entire time as she yelled at me to stop as it was too late for crying now. My grandmother sat silently through it all and I knew she felt my hurt. We had that type of connection. As I sat in the backseat, I began to think of all the good times I had shared with my grand-mother as a little girl and all the love she showed me, how much my little brother's looked up to me and how my little sister would not re-ally understand why my belly was getting larger. I thought of the embarrassment and shame I would face at school and bring to my family and how my plans for college would be over. I recall thinking I would run away, but where would I run? Then I thought maybe just kill yourself, no one loves you anyway. It's odd but at the moment of thinking that, my grandmother turned around and looked at me from the front seat. It's as if she felt what I was thinking. Her ex-pression said it all and I knew that if I was indeed pregnant, I would make it somehow.

I was so hurt that day as the doctor confirmed our suspicions. Although I knew, I was hoping it was only a bad dream and I would wake up in the doctor's office and he would say, Mrs. London, your daughter has a stomach virus or chicken pox, the mumps, measles, rubella, anything but she's pregnant! Unfortunately, it did not happen that way.

My mom questioned if I knew whose it was and I stated that it was Patrick's. I explained to her what had happened, however, she did not believe that he had forced himself on me. I had been raped, but because I liked the guy who raped me, to her it wasn't considered rape. I never told another person about how Patrick forced himself on me because I felt that they would not believe me either.

My mother never made contact with either Patrick or his family to tell them the news. I did. He didn't believe me at first, then he denied that it was his. So now not only did my mother call me a whore, in so many words, so did the father of my child. The first and only person I told about the pregnancy, even before him, was my best friend, Deborah. When I told her she was shocked but like a true friend, she did not judge me or make me feel worse than I already did. Instead, she vowed to stick with me through it all and be the god-mother of my baby. She also kept my secret, now that's a true friend.

Ironically, about four months later my mother went to the doctor. Strange as it was, she was pregnant too!! That tripped everybody out, mother and daughter both pregnant. I was seventeen and she was thirty-two. We both went to Stuttgart for our doctor appointments and even had the same doctor. I embraced the news of my mother's pregnancy in hopes that it would take some of the pressure off of me and luckily it did.

> **St. Luke 1:42** "....Blessed art thou among women,
> and blessed is the fruit of thy womb."

You Have A Bouncing Baby Boy!

I finished out my eleventh grade year without anyone besides my best friend Deborah knowing I was pregnant. I was on the basketball team and still practiced during the off season. I was small in stature with only a small bulge by May. Things between my mother and I weren't as strained as they had been and I even think she may have been a little excited about the baby. My younger sister was now an active (bad) five-year-old, so a new baby would be a nice addition, mainly because as I got bigger, she terrorized me as much as possible. Whenever I made her mad she would taunt me with "big belly, big belly." I would chase her around and around the house and my mom would make me stop. I can still see her little face over in the corner holding her mouth laughing. When my mom was not there, she paid the price for her taunts. After school ended for the summer, I got a summer job working at the school doing janitorial stuff. I needed the money to help get things for the baby who I was already thinking of names for. I was still concealing my pregnancy from my boss and co-workers and managed to get away with it the entire summer.

Then August rolled around and school began again, the girdle was no longer doing the trick. Everyone was shocked to learn that I was pregnant. I was an honor student and pretty popular. There had been a few others at the small school we attended who had gotten pregnant, but it still was uncommon to see pregnant teenage girls.

My pregnancy, however, was pretty normal in spite of the shame of walking around with a growing belly. At the beginning of the school year we took our senior pictures and I had to wear a very tight girdle in order not to show. Despite the girdle, I could still tell in my proofs that I was pregnant since I was now five months and had a nice size little lump. My teachers were supportive, especially Mrs. Eason, my Home Economics teacher. Mrs. Eason hosted a baby shower for me and I got so much stuff to help prepare for the baby's arrival. I believe that was when reality truly set in and I realized I was having a baby!

Eventually Patrick began to acknowledge that the child was his, mainly because he and the mother of his other child were no longer together and he was living with a friend of his ex. To put the icing on the cake, rumor had it that Patrick had another girl pregnant. He was also sneaking around with yet another. While we walked around mad at each other like fools, he continued in the pleasure of sneaking around with all of us.

It was strange, but the bigger my belly grew the deeper I seemed to fall in love with the baby and care for its father. Although Patrick and I did not have any real contact other than on occasion. Oddly enough though, I still hoped that we could be together and raise our child, but he was doing everything contrary to planning a future for us. I guess every woman wants that happily ever after with their child's father, yet so few at the age of 17 actually get it. After all he was not with his other child's mother and there were supposedly two others in my shoes. It was summertime and I had most people fooled about my true feelings for him, but Deborah knew. She knew me better than anyone.

As months passed and my stomach grew larger, I was preparing for the baby, yet I was getting scared. I knew where the baby had to come from, but it just did not add up how something possibly weighing seven pounds, according to my doctor, was going to manage to come from there. The time was drawing near for me to have the baby and I had not spoken to Patrick in months. I had listened to his lies and eventually got tired as I waited for the birth of my son in December. Inside I was hurting because Patrick wasn't standing by my side through all of this, but on the outside I was hard as steel – I was angry! Revenge was on mind though I never let anyone see me sweat. Still, when I was alone at night, rubbing my protruding belly, I would cry silently into my pillow.

Genesis 3:16 "Unto the woman he said,
I will greatly multiply they sorrow and thy conception,
in sorrow thou shalt bring forth children..."

That's My Boy!

My son Corey was born on December 1, 1981. He was so beautiful. Thankfully he did not weigh seven pounds, but instead five pounds and five ounces. My labor had been very long and scary and I had been pretty mean to the nurse that had wanted me to walk around. I did not feel like walking and if Patrick had been there I would have pulled his eyelashes out. Yet, after the labor was over and I heard my baby cry for the first time and laid eyes on his beautiful face, it was as if all of my pain seemed to quickly fade and I was in love. He looked just like Patrick who did not have a clue that my sweet Corey had been born. We took him home after a few days and everyone showered him with love. Every day I dressed him like he was one of the baby dolls I used to play with. However, I quickly found out that he was not a doll. I once had a Baby Alive doll and when I turned her off or took her batteries out, she would stop crying or pooping or whatever. Corey was not like that, he did not come with batteries and I could not remove the batteries and put him in my shoebox under the bed like I did my dolls. He was a living, breathing creature that needed his mother to love and care for him. Sometimes the thought would overwhelm me but my mother was always there teaching me how to care for him. About three weeks after Corey's birth, I got a message that Patrick wanted to come see him. At first I was reluctant but eventually agreed. Patrick didn't bring a bag of pampers, a rattle or a bottle – all he brought was himself. The expression on his face was priceless as he stared at his son. He sat there and held him for hours without saying a word. Those 3 or 4 hours would end up being the longest period of time that he would end up spending with his son at one time during his childhood. Within a few months, Patrick's daughter, Corey's baby sister, was born. A year later the other young lady he had been sneaking around with gave birth to his second daughter.

Within the next few months, Patrick's two other children were born, both girls. Now Patrick had fathered two girls and two boys and was only around twenty years old himself.

I named Corey after my grandmother Cora because he was her first great grandchild. She and my mother loved him so much and everyone in the family thought he was the most beautiful child. Although Corey was conceived by what is considered a "date rape" these days, he was a blessing to me from day one, bringing me joy and a sense of purpose. With Corey only a few weeks old, we all spent our first Christmas at my grandmother's house to celebrate the new addition to the family. My grandmother was as proud as she could be as she held her first great-grandchild and was especially thrilled that he was named in her honor. I have since learned that although the act of getting pregnant unmarried was not pleasing to God, the child was a blessing from God. At that time, I did not know either.

The Christmas break was soon over and I returned to school to finish my senior year. I had been doing my school work at home in order to keep up prior to the break, but was glad to finally be back with my peers. The hardest part of my day was leaving my baby every morning. Yet, the greatest part was coming back home to him every afternoon.

Shortly after Corey was born, I do not exactly recall how old Corey was at the time, the new rumor was that Patrick was getting married to his ex-girlfriend's former best friend. As it turned out, they were not just rumors. Patrick did get married. One Sunday afternoon while walking down the street with Deborah, Patrick pulled alongside of us in his car with "just married" on the back of it. He was blowing his horn and carrying on like a public fool. Deb looked at me and I looked at her, we both knew if I had a bomb, I would've sent all of us to hell that day. Right then I vowed that he would pay for all the pain he had put me through. I began to medicate my disappointment and anger with my other love, marijuana. *"I'm in love with Mary Jane–she's my main thang–she makes me feel alright–she make my heart sang..."* (Rick James)

Proverbs 27:3 "A stone is heavy, and the sand weighty, but a fool's wrath is heavier than them both."

Graduation Day

In May 1982 I walked across the stage to receive my high school diploma and graduated with honors. It was not always easy to study and take care of my son, but I worked hard and stayed focused. Graduating was the second proudest moment in my life next to having my son. I knew I would continue in high school after getting pregnant, but my plans for college had been abandoned. I wanted to try and make a life for my child and me. Thus, I needed a good job. As I was leaving the gymnasium, I handed the graduation carnation given to me to my five month old son whom my mother was holding. Meanwhile, my dad was holding my one month old brother, Courtney, who was born on April 4th.

My parents babysat the night after graduation to allow me the opportunity to go out and celebrate with my friends. We headed to a club, P.J's, which was about 45 minutes away. There had been several graduations that day, so the place was packed. I thought that I would faint when Deborah and I ran into my Arkansas Razorback crush, U.S. Reed. He was just as fine in person as he was running up and down the basketball court on my television. I loved me some U.S. Reed! The girls and I had a lot of fun that night as we danced the night away. It felt so good to have graduated high school on schedule and it felt even better to be out that night with my friends. It ended up being a very late night and we all returned to Dewitt to spend the night with Deborah's brother and wife. We were all spending the weekend with them so we hung out that Saturday and partied again that night. Unfortunately, my party had come to an end and I had to go home that night. Sunday morning as the sun was shining into my bedroom window and a small hangover was making me feel queasy, I awoke to the sounds of my baby crying. It was official. I was now a full time mother.

Colossians 3:20 "Children, obey your parents in all things, for this is well pleasing unto the Lord."

My Departure

Throughout my senior year I had been telling everyone that after graduation I would be moving to Kentucky to start a new life for myself and Corey. My mom had suggested keeping Corey until I got settled, partly to help me out and partly because she was so in love with him and my baby brother Courtney. She would dress them like twins most times because they looked a lot alike. The plan was for me to stay with my uncle and aunt until I was able to get my own place. I always loved Louisville as a child, so the thought of living there as an adult was exciting.

The weekend before I was to leave I was out celebrating with my friends in one of our hangout spots. While out someone informed me that Patrick was around and wanted to talk with me. He droned on about me leaving and how he did not want me to go. Blah, blah, blah! He was still married, but he and his wife were on bad terms at the time.

He suggested that we get away and spend one last night together – we did. On that night, I knew something was different and the tables were turning in my favor. I could tell his concern for me was genuine as he promised to come to Kentucky and visit me.

Although I still liked Patrick a lot, I was no longer in love with him. Time had healed some wounds I thought. Changed, now I felt it was my time to run the show. For the first time in my life I felt

43

empowered as a woman. I was a mother and moving out on my own, leaving my comfort zone and starting a new life. If that's all it would have taken, then I would have had it made, but the world was much larger than I had anticipated and there was more to life than getting high, having sex and drinking. I had a son now – I had responsibilities. I had to try and make some things happen. Unfortunately, I also had a little too much free time on my hands in Louisville before Corey was to come and things didn't quite work out the way I planned.

      Genesis 4:7 "If thou doest well, shalt thou be accepted? And if thou doest not well, sin lieth at the door..."

Why Do Fools Fall in Love?

I moved to Louisville Kentucky in May 1982 to stay with my aunt and uncle. I did not know that they had separated, but my Aunt Linda still allowed me to stay in the home with her and their three young sons. I helped her out by babysitting when the youngest was not in the daycare. I also made sure the two school age children got off to school and greeted them when they returned home. I did not have a job, but I did apply for assistance with the state in order to have money for Corey's arrival. My aunt was now a single mother and a nurse at Norton's Hospital. I admired her strong will and work ethic and I tried not to be too much of a bother or burden while living with her.

My mother reluctantly sent Corey to me about two months after I had settled into Louisville and a few weeks after he arrived, believe it or not, Patrick kept his promise of coming to visit. Patrick came to visit me with a family friend who was dating my cousin Gina, whom I had started hanging with since Tanya no longer lived in Kentucky. Needless to say, I was excited and surprised to see him. I asked about his wife and he explained that they had separated and she was staying with her mother. When the weekend ended and they had to leave I was sad, but Gina and I made plans to drive to Arkansas a few weeks later to visit them. I was equally as excited about the forthcoming trip because it would give me a chance to see my family.

Sure enough a few weeks later Gina and I drove to Arkansas and when I arrived I saw my family and Patrick. Though Patrick and wife had gotten back together, a few days before my arrival he had made her upset and she had gone to her mother's house. It would turn out to be an ongoing thing. Patrick and his friend would visit us. We would visit them while the wife would go home to her mother. The bodacious thing about it was most times I stayed at the house that Patrick shared with his wife. The home belonged to his elderly grandmother so he and I both felt that since the house had been given to him, he could have whomever he chose to be there. On one occasion, I was there for about two weeks during the holidays. People began to tell me they knew when I was coming home because the wife was at her mother's.

I felt my actions were justified because I had a son by him. I also didn't mind messing up his "happy" home since I felt he owed me, if it meant being uncomfortable for a while, so what? My feelings had grown stronger and even the way Corey was conceived didn't seem to bother me anymore. However, the fact that he was married did. My actions were revengeful and I was enjoying every minute of it. He told me that he wanted to settle down with me. Wasn't that called bigamy? I didn't believe a word. By this point, I was so used to being lied to by men that nothing he said really mattered.

Once when I was visiting him in Arkansas, I was at his house when his wife and some of her family members came to get some of her things. I stood there in the living room as she walked past and got some things. Her sister was inside with her as her brothers waited outside. As she left the house, she said something to Patrick and they started yelling at each other. The next thing I knew, Patrick was chasing the truck she was riding in down the street while she sat back laughing at him. On another occasion, I realized the danger I was putting my life in by staying with Patrick on my visits. Patrick and I had been away from the house and when we returned a basket that belonged to her was gone. This could only mean she still had a key to the house or had broken in. I remember thinking, she could come in here and shoot me and would be justified, but at that time I was fearless. It is true–God watches over fools.

Psalm 91:11 "For he shall give his angels charge over thee, to keep thee in all thy ways."

The Chapter Ends

*E*ventually, Patrick and I both got tired of running up and down the highway. Arkansas was our common ground, but I didn't like the long distance relationship, especially knowing that it held no future for me and my son. Patrick was the same selfish person he had always been, but I went to see him one more time before it was finally over. I had gone down and as usual, Patrick had either put his wife out or she had simply left, depends on who you ask. It just so happened that her mom lived in the same projects as my aunt. On my second day in town Patrick picked me up and gave me his car, a black Delta '88, to use until he got off work. While driving around and chilling with my friend, Deborah and Corey, we stopped to get gas at a station ironically right behind the house where his wife's mother lived. As I was pulling off, I heard a crash and looked back to see Patrick's wife running toward the car throwing bottles. I pulled out of the lot and proceeded to drive away. I heard her mom, who also was heading towards the gas station, yelling, "You should have thrown a d_ _ _ brick!" The incident hadn't fazed me as I continued to drive the car around. It was only when my grandmother got wind and asked me to take the car back to Patrick that I did.

After taking the car back, Deborah and I went out walking. We went to the park and his wife with about ten other girls came down there. We walked up the streets – they all came up there. I could hear her talking trash and them urging her to confront me, but she never got the guts to just come to me.

Finally Deb and I went to my aunt's house, in the projects where Patrick's wife's mother and grandfather also lived, and she followed us back down there with her crew. Two of my other aunts had gotten off work at the factory where Patrick also worked at and had stopped by also. When Deborah and I were attempting to leave with them, the wife yelled something at me that I ignored. However, when I got in the car, she stuck up her middle finger at me and my aunt looked at me and said "Do you want her?" Of course I did, so we stopped on the side of the street by her grandfather's house where she was and she headed towards the car. I was trying to get out in such a hurry that I forgot I had Corey in my lap and dropped him. He landed on his butt. My other aunt got the baby and I headed toward the wife. We locked up midway in her grandfather's backyard and I handled my business. Her male cousin came out after a few minutes and tried to break us up by telling us Patrick was no good and we were both fools for fighting over him. I knew he was telling the truth, but only after I got her in a position where she could not move did I let her go and then it was over. Just like the fight was over, so was the *"Patrick Chapter"* in my life. I felt I had accomplished everything I had wanted to accomplish. There was no love for Patrick anymore and I was done.

Thinking back, that was one of the craziest times of my life. It wasn't the wife I had wanted to hurt, she had only gotten caught up in the crossfire. Years later I would apologize to her and thankfully she accepted. Unfortunately, it would be after getting a taste of my very own medicine. I returned to Louisville ready to begin a new life.

Proverbs 7:26 "For by means of a whorish woman a man is brought to a piece of bread, and the adulteress will hunt for the precious life"

~Chapter III*~*

Why Do Good Girls Love Bad Boys?

hortly after my return to Kentucky, Leasa, my aunt's other niece arrived. It was on!!! We were the same age and though we were never close friends since we went to different schools, all of that changed very quickly. Corey was back and forth living with my mother and me during this time. Since I didn't have a place of my own, my mom tried to help out by keeping him from time to time. As soon as Leasa got settled in, she started asking our aunt for the car, something I was afraid to ask. Leasa would ask because she was my aunt's biological niece and had grown up with her, I was only related to her through marriage and was not as comfortable. We started going to the park on Sundays and to the Broadway skating rink on Friday and Saturday nights. We did everything teenagers do and had a ball. Sometimes I would get my Uncle Charlie's car and we would drive it all over the city. Other times we would have just the "pinto" with its broken door and all. God surely was watching over us because once we were so "happy" (interpretation–high!) that Leasa entered the interstate on the exit ramp! After she got situated and managed to back off before someone killed us, we laughed, but it truly wasn't funny initially.

The skating rink is where I met Kav. It was a Friday night and I was on my way to the restroom when this guy, dressed in pimp attire, with an entourage of girls and guys walked past me. He looked me dead in the eyes and declared, "I like that." He smiled and all I could see was gold teeth. I walked past him wondering to whom was this pimp speaking. Later as Leasa and I were enjoying watching the groups skate "trio," he approached me and introduced himself as Kav. I lied and told him my name was "Rebecca," which was my pseudonym for people who I didn't want to know my real name. After talking and laughing with him for a while, Leasa and I began to enjoy his company. I asked him if he was a pimp and he denied it, but that at one time he had been considered a pimp. He gave me his number and I gave him my cousin's number. He asked where I lived and I lied and gave him my cousin's address. It turned out he knew my cousin and lived right around the corner.

I enjoyed talking to Kav because he was funny and Leasa liked tripping off of him too. So after a few weeks of talking on the phone, we began a relationship. Leasa wasn't dating anyone during this time and Kav had a lot of cousins. Eventually he hooked Leasa up with the one they all called "Man." Little did I know, I was dating a "gangsta" in every sense of the word and Leasa was dating the cousin of a "gangsta." By the time we found out it was too late. After a few weeks, one of my male cousins began to tell me about Kav and his "crew" and how they had been in jail numerous times for fighting and stealing and everything in between. The Crips and Bloods didn't have anything on Kav and his crew. When I asked Kav about it, he did not deny it and on more than one occasion I witnessed his awful temper.

Our sexual relationship began at his mother's home where he lived. I was nineteen years old and he was twenty-two. I thought, maybe this is the one–the one that is going to love me and only me.

After all there were lots of girls there the night we met but he chose me. It amazes me how people's paths cross for a divine purpose and yet we have no idea initially. With Kav I learned how it was possible to hurt and be satisfied at the same time. He also reiterated the fact that all men were not created equal. He was as gentle with me as possible and after the act he did something that no one had previously done, he talked. For what seemed like hours, he talked about himself, his family and what attracted him to me. I noticed a huge Ziploc bag full of folded pieces of paper and asked him what it was. He explained that the bag held phone numbers of women he met at the skating rink on Friday and Saturday nights. He promised to get rid of the bag once we became serious, but I don't believe he ever did. As I got to know him better over the following months, I understood how he was able to get all those numbers. He had a charm about him and he was also a big liar.

On several occasions I tried breaking up with him for lying. I eventually found out he was cheating also. His old habits were proving to be hard to break although he swore to me that he was through being a player. Our relationship was complicated. Despite how we would stop talking or be upset with each other, he always made it clear to me that I was his woman and nothing was going to change that. My cousins had all warned me about him and my other family members did not like him, but a mixture of fear and infatuation kept me with him. One evening Kav picked me up from my aunt's and we were just riding around town after going to his mom's house and doing the usual, not a lot of talking but a lot of everything else. Kav did not smoke weed and did not like the fact that I did, so that was out. I was ready to go home and roll up the remainder of the weed I had saved for the next day. I had not been able to reach him on several occasions earlier in the week, so I was still somewhat perturbed. As we rode, I sat in silence, wondering who had been in the place I had just laid earlier that week. I did not have the courage to tell him that I strongly suspected that he was seeing someone else. Although I was more than 99% sure that he was cheating, I could not fully bear the thought of not having him in my life. I tried to convince myself that I could change him and often tried to figure out what more could I do to keep his mind off other women. I found it to be a huge and impossible task, there was nothing that I could do to keep someone that did not want to be kept. I had made up my mind earlier that day that I was going to break up with him. After I arriving at his mother's home, I decided that it would not be a good idea to do so there because I knew he would probably flip out and I did not want to be over there all night arguing. All of a sudden as we were riding, it just came out. I told him I wanted to break up. He was talking at the time I interrupted and suddenly got quiet but continued to drive. I noticed we weren't heading toward my house as we turned down an alley. Needless to say, I began to get scared. I looked over at him and he was biting his lower lip, a sign that he was angry. Stopping the car, he went under his seat and pulled out a gun. All of the things my cousin had told me about Kav flashed through my mind and I felt my life was about to be over. I was going to die right there in that alley.

People had told me that he had killed one or more persons before and had beaten countless others to near death. When we were together, I only saw the gentle side most times, but I could tell there was something beneath the surface. Waving the gun in my face, he proclaimed, "If I can't have you no one will." Feverishly he fidgeted with the window switches. My window had been up and when he pressed the switch it went down. He pointed the gun in my direction and pulled the trigger. My left ear went deaf. As I sat there in disbelief, with my one good ear I heard him say "_ _ _ _." I thought that window was up! He was trying to shoot the window out! He continued talking and yelling and all I could do was sit there as my other ear went deaf from the close range blast. Eventually he drove out of the alley and headed toward my house. The ride was both long and silent.

When Kav and I arrived in front of the house I reached for my door, trying to get out in a hurry, and he grabbed my arm. My hearing was slowly coming back. He feigned an apology and when I jerked my arm away, he pulled the gun out again. I got out of the car anyway and walked the longest walk of my life to the steps of my aunt's house. I expected to hear another gunshot, but instead I heard him drive away. I went upstairs to my bed, still in shock and tried to figure out how I would escape this madman. There would be one more incident where Kav would fire his gun to intimidate me. The next time he shot the baseboard of the car. Shortly after we had begun dating, Kav went to jail for something. His being in and out of jail occurred several times during our relationship. Not only were Kav and his crew ruthless, they were also thieves. Not nickel and dime thieves but truck load of furniture thieves. He also had a love for motorcycles and that love almost got all of us killed one night. Allegedly, Kav and his crew stole a Mexican motorcycle gangs' motorcycles, broke them down to the brake pads and hid the parts. Somehow the Mexicans found out who had their bikes and while Kav and I were riding around with his friend Ernest and my cousin's girl-friend, some members of the gang stopped our car and confronted them. The girlfriend and I sat in the car as Kav stood against a vacant building with his arms crossed. Ernest stood with a gun being pointed at his head. There was a lot of yelling and then we saw another guy pull out his gun. We were parked by a hill and immediately began plotting our escape route. It was only after we heard the first gun shot that we hit the locks–unlocking the car doors and jumped out leaving the car and them behind. We did not leave completely but managed to get on the other side of the hill and peep over. I had not been so afraid in my life. I just knew I was about to be a witness to a murder, even worst I thought of the possibility of them getting rid of the witnesses. I loved action movies but did not want to be the main character in one. Luckily they came to some type of agreement and the motorcycles ended up back to their owners. We rode all over the city collecting the "alleged" stolen parts. Some were hidden in parks, in large green garbage bags that had been strategically sunken down into the lakes, others were elsewhere. The ending to that situation could have been worst, but Kav and his crew were pretty slick. Having had enough, a week or two later I was relieved to hear from one of his cousins that Kav had gotten locked up once again.

I had been considering going back to Arkansas for a while to escape Kav but didn't have the money. In jail, he called repeatedly asking me to visit him and eventually I did. Once Leasa went with me and we ended up having to walk all the way back home from the downtown jail. When we finally made it home, Leasa was so tired she stepped out of her shoes and into the bed. One shoe was in front of the other as if she was still walking. We both laughed so hard and then fell asleep exhausted. Leasa and I continued to have a lot of adventures with Kav and Man after he got of jail. We would meet up at the skating rink and down at the Belvedere, but mostly at the house – sorry Aunt Linda. Still, after saving for what seemed like forever, I finally had enough money to attempt an escape from Kav by going back to Arkansas. It was the perfect time to leave because Kav was locked up again. But as usual, there was just one problem.

Though Kav was in and out of jail, we maintained an active sex life and during his most recent jail visit, I realized I had not had a period in a couple months. I was hoping it was just stress until the so-called "stress" started making my belly bigger. I wasn't sure how many months I was, but I estimated about three. Kav and I had talked about having a baby together a lot because he had met and fallen in love with Corey, which made him want a son of his own. He often asked me to stop taking birth control and get pregnant. So after I ran out of pills, I had stopped taking them. The pregnancy was confirmed and after initially being caught up in the fantasy that having a baby with him would keep him, reality set in and I realized that the majority of the time I had known Kav, he had been in jail. My child's father was a jailbird in every sense of the word. Now not only was I craving for his love, but his love through our child. One day Kav called from jail and I told him I was pregnant. He did not believe me at first. It was at that point that he finally told me he had a little girl named Brandy. Here I was thinking I was having his first child and he already had one that he had been keeping secret from me the entire time. I felt betrayed and briefly questioned whether I would keep the baby or not. When I expressed those feelings to him, he got very agitated and told me that he still wanted a son and that there would be more than one life lost if I did anything other than giving birth. Read between the lines, I did. I proceeded to tell him the rest of my news regarding me moving back to Arkansas, which didn't go over so well. He did not like the fact that I was pregnant with his child and leaving the state. That was one time that I was grateful he was locked up. He asked me to visit him before I left and I did with Leasa. I was already showing so he knew I wasn't lying. We talked briefly and I could not help but cry as I left. Not realizing the reason I hurt was because my soul was intertwined with his soul.

Things between Kav and I were never the same after that. I still had not discovered true love. I thought having the baby would fill the void I was still carrying in my heart, but I soon found out that I was wrong.

I John 4:18 "There is no fear in love,
but perfect love casteth out fear: because fear hath torment.
He that feareth is not made perfect in love."

Return to the Natural State

I reluctantly returned to Arkansas to have my second baby. I knew I did not want to be there permanently, but at the time it was best for me. I rented a little place and my family helped me out a lot. Patrick was still around doing the same things he had always been doing but I no longer cared. Corey and I mainly stayed in the house waiting on my due date to roll around. I finally had Corey all to myself and he had just turned two, so I was enjoying spending time with him. Although I was pregnant, I still had a habit that I had not broken which was smoking marijuana. Money was scarce, unbelievably I was missing Kav and I did not want to be in Arkansas–my excuses to smoke. There was a drug dealer in town that would let me get single joints on credit so I was able to feed my habit. I did not see marijuana as being as harmful as cocaine or heroin, so I continued to smoke throughout the pregnancy. It occasionally occurred to me that smoking would harm my baby and I would feel guilty, yet my selfish desires to feel better over ruled my common sense most times.

On February 18th, 1984 I turned twenty. My mom, stepdad, and my brothers had come to my place to celebrate my birthday. We had a great time and I drank a couple beers even. Around 5:00 a.m. while everyone was asleep I began having sharp pains. I woke my step-dad and told him I thought I was going into labor. We all jumped in the car and headed to the hospital. Because the pains weren't that bad, I began to think it was a false alarm. We arrived at the hospital and I was admitted. The nurse checked me and could feel the head – I was about to deliver any moment. She kept telling me not to push but I couldn't help it. The baby was pushing itself out. By the time the doctor arrived, the head was coming out already and he simply stood at the end of the table to prepare when she sprang out! We all tripped out! It was a girl and when I looked at her, she looked just like Kav. She was a little bitty thing, only 6lbs 1oz. Later I called and told Kav, though he was disappointed that she was not a boy, nevertheless he was excited. I named her Tashona because it was similar to my name.

After I had Tashona, I stayed in Arkansas for almost four months before returning to Kentucky to let her daddy see her. After living in Louisville, being back in that small town was not where I wanted be other than to see my family and my best friend, Deborah. The summer had come and Kav and I had previously discussed my returning to Louisville for the summer so his family could see the baby and the two of us possibly staying permanently. One month later, Tashona and I boarded the bus and headed to Kentucky. She cried almost the entire way. It seemed like nothing I did would comfort her. I know other passengers wanted to throw both of us off. At one point I went into the bathroom and she was still crying. I looked at the toilet and then looked at her and figured, nah, someone will notice that I didn't come back out with her. I'm telling the truth! That is how aggravated I had grown by her crying. It was a long twelve hour ride. Finally we made it and one of Kav's family members picked us up and took us to her house.

It was hours before Kav arrived to the house although he knew we were there waiting. I was getting upset because these were family members I did not know and I felt awkward there with them. When Kav finally arrived he acted strange. It had only been a year since we had seen each other, yet I didn't feel much love.

> **1 John 3:18** "My little children, let us not love in word, neither in tongue, but in deed and in truth."

Another Closed Chapter

I stayed in Louisville maybe a month, mainly with Kav's family because he was now secretly dating someone else. Sometimes he would come and check on Tashona and me. He would take us down the street to where some friends of his lived with a lot of large dogs inside the house. It was the nastiest house and whenever we would leave I would have to get dog hair off of our clothes and poop off of my shoes. Then Kav took us out to Newberg. It was far from my cousins and other family, but at least the house was clean. I never really knew the people, with whom we were staying, but they were gone most times and so was Kav. I kept to myself, staying in the room with the baby without a TV or radio, and staring at the walls. When I finally was able to get from out there, I tried never to look back. I eventually rode back to Arkansas with my cousins for their yearly trip on the 4th of July.

Returning to Arkansas, I didn't have a place to stay so I stayed with my parents for a while. I was miserable so after a few months Tashona and I went back to Louisville. My mom kept Corey again and gave me another chance to get myself together. When I arrived in Louisville, I stayed with my cousins for a little while and then with friends, Jackie and Tammy, whom I had met through Kav. They looked at Kav as their brother and immediately accepted Tashona and me into the family. They lived with their mom, Ms. Elliot, who willingly opened her home to me. Before long, I affectionately called her momma. She treated all of Jackie and Tammy's friends like they were her own children. During this time I smoked weed pretty regularly, but it was also in Ms. Elliot's house, at a house party, that I had my first experience with cocaine. A friend of Jackie, Tammy, and Kav's who was also a drug dealer came to the party. He also snorted his own product and asked me if I wanted to sample his cocaine. Once I agreed, we went into the bathroom and he showed me how to do it. The high I experienced was greater than any high I had ever had previously. I sat through the party and after the party was well over, I was still sitting. The next morning I was still sitting. It was late into the next evening before I finally went to sleep. It was a nice high, but I didn't like the paranoid feeling it left me with, thus, it wasn't something I cared to try again.

Every weekend Tammy and Jackie either had a party or other friends of theirs would come over and we'd do something. Momma and her boyfriend Lucky worked at the bar down the street on the weekends, so we were always having fun. One particular incident I experienced while I was staying there was not very much fun though. Kav had taken me on the other side of town to get my hair styled. I wasn't familiar with the area, but was glad that I was finally getting something done to my head. It was during the 80's so of course that meant a fresh curl, the hairdo that left pillows greasy and heads inactivated drrrrry. After getting my fresh curl Kav still had not arrived to pick me up. It was dark by now and that part of town seemed very busy with activity. It was a Friday night and people were hanging out on the corners and in yards. A guy approached me and I thought I recognized him as one of Kav's friends, so I spoke to him. I asked him if he had seen Kav come by and he said no. After making small talk for a few minutes he told me that he lived down the street a little bit and I could use his phone to call Kav. This being the age before cell phones, I agreed but only after he told me his mother and sister were at the house also.

I walked down to the house but after getting in and sitting down I never heard anyone else. I noticed how he had locked the door behind him after coming in the house, but did not think much of it until later. I asked him if I could use his restroom before using the phone and he directed me down the hallway. It was only after I got in the restroom that I realized I had left my purse in the chair in the living room where I had been sitting. When I returned to the living room, I immediately noticed that my purse was no longer in the chair where I had left it. I asked him where my purse was and he said that he had not seen it. I knew something was not right and only wanted to get out of there. All of a sudden, fear came over me and I thought the guy would hurt me. My instincts told me to play it cool and go with the flow until I could find a way of escape. I asked him about using the phone and he immediately got off of the subject by asking if I wanted a drink. In order to stall, I said yes and he went in the kitchen. I got up to try and run out, but before my mind could tell my feet to move, he was back in the room with me. He told me that there wasn't any more beer in the fridge so he would run down to the corner and grab us a couple. I tried to go with him, but he insisted that I stay and wait for him. Still playing along with him, I said okay knowing that there would be tread marks on his carpet by me high-tailing it out of there as soon as he left. To my surprise, I heard him lock the door from the outside locking me in when he left. I panicked and began running around looking for my purse, realizing that there was no one else in the house. I ran in the kitchen and saw that the backdoor had what looked like twenty locks on it. I figured by the time I unlocked all of those locks he would have been back so I went to the window. It was a fairly big jump, but I did not care. I jumped and must have rolled what seemed like fifty feet before I was able to get up and run like a bat out of hell.

I was in unfamiliar territory and quickly ended up in a park. I did not know which park I was in because it was so dark. It had also rained earlier that day so the ground was muddy. Trying to get as far away from the area as possible, I was running and walking, falling and rolling all through that park. Eventually I made it to the street, which turned into a long winding road. I stayed close to the side trying not to get hit, when a car stopped. Inside of the car was an older man who rolled down the window and asked if I needed a ride. All I could vocalize was "please help me" as I began to cry. He looked at me and seeing how muddy I was, replied, "I don't want any trouble" and sped away.

I continued to cry and walk for what seemed like hours before I came to Algonquin Parkway. I finally knew where I was but still miles from Jackie and Tammy's house and did not have a dime to my name. All of my money, identification and a small amount of weed were in my purse that had mysteriously disappeared. I continued to walk until at last I made it. As I walked up I saw Kav standing outside with everyone else – he had been looking for me. I was so relieved to see him and so tired from the walk, that all I could do was stand in front of him and cry. I told him what happened and he got so angry. After asking if I remembered which house it was, he told me to change while he called a couple of his cousins. I got dressed, went outside, and saw Kav with his cousins putting something in the back of his car. We all loaded in the car and headed across town.

By now the streets were quiet, we arrived on the block of the house and we parked down the street from it. Kav and his cousins went to stake out the place to see if anyone was in the house. When they saw that no one was there, they went in through the window I had jumped out of hours earlier. They began looking for my purse, but could not find out. They came back to the car and went into the trunk and got glass bottles, old rags and gasoline–gas bombs. They took and strategically placed the bottles throughout the house and within minutes it went up in smoke. Kav and his cousins ran back to the car and we sat watching the house burn to the ground as the police and fire trucks arrived. I sat in silence watching a small crowd gather as flames shot into the air. The house must have been burning about 5 minutes when I saw the man bursting through the crowd. He just stood there watching his house burn. I was glad that it was burning – he had stolen my identification, my money, my weed! As Kav and his cousins began to laugh, so did I. Whenever I was around them, I felt like I was invincible. I was Bonnie and Kav was Clyde, I was his ride or die chick though not always by choice. They were a devious and conniving crew, driven by their own lies and deceit and I was becoming just like them. It's true, whatever you feed your heart and soul the most of, is what it will become.

Jeremiah 17:9 "The heart is deceitful above all things and desperately wicked: who can know it?"

Moving On

$\mathcal{E}$ventually I was able to rent my own little one bedroom duplex. Shortly after, Jackie got pregnant and gave birth to my god-son DeRomeo with me in the delivery room. These days I was barely surviving on welfare and food stamps. The only good times I experienced during this period, was the times spent with my Louisville family. Every now and then I would either go to either my uncle or cousin's houses. Kav and I definitely were not dating anymore. I had grown tired of his lies and of the long nights wondering if he was in jail or out of jail. He had a girlfriend that was older than himself that he had obviously fallen in love with. I don't believe he ever stopped being a cheater but he had deep feelings for her and his actions showed me that. Naturally in the beginning I was hurt, yet instead of saying "okay, sit down, regroup and stop expecting someone to love you", I met and began talking to a guy named Michael.

Michael was from a large family and lived around the corner from me. I actually met him at the basketball court at the Boy's and Girl's Club. I still loved playing basketball and after moving in the neighborhood I would often be found at the court. Michael was sweet and really good looking. At the time we met, he was dating someone who had a son by him. Michael's mother, who was mean as a rattlesnake when she was drinking but okay when she was sober, liked the other girl more than me. Therefore, neither she nor his sisters were happy when Michael and I began dating. They viewed me as a hood rat with two kids and the other girl as their nephew's mother. Of course this caused instant drama. Michael and I had our good days and bad days. We got high all the time, but not in front of the kids. Most times they were not with me but in Arkansas with my mom.

Michael was a pretty laid back, quiet guy but was not the most law abiding citizen in Louisville. Michael was a small time drug dealer, mainly dealing to provide for his children. I always thought that we smoked more than he sold although he claimed otherwise. Michael was also a thief.

At this point in my life I wasn't going anywhere. It was as if I was going to be on welfare all my life. Jobs were scarce and even if I had one, the childcare would have eaten up everything I potentially would earn. All of the programs young girls have now were not available then. Resultantly, I always wasn't able to pay the rent and eventually was evicted. The same night that I was evicted, Michael was arrested for possession of a stolen vehicle. My once good friend Jackie had gotten angry with me because her boyfriend, who was also Kav's cousin, lied saying we had slept together. Although I denied it, she believed him and we became enemies. I had grown behind on my $90.00 per month rent and the landlord had gotten me served with eviction papers but did not show up to court. Since he was a no show, the court gave me thirty days to move.

One night Jackie and her boyfriend tried to come into the house and Michael put a gun out the window. Angry, they called the police. Somehow Jackie had spoken to my landlord about renting the place and he had provided her a lease. Since she now had a lease and I didn't, they made me leave. They began bringing my things out and sitting them on the sidewalk. As this was happening, they also were handcuffing Michael for the stolen car that was parked out front. I could do nothing but cry as I gathered my things. A lady who lived across the street came and got the children and helped me move my stuff into her living room. She allowed us to spend the night in her place, but it could not be permanent. The next day I went and spoke to a lady around the corner who had a big house that she lived in with her two children. We were not really friends, but I told her my situation and she let me move in with them temporarily. Though I cannot remember her name, God knows, and I pray that He has blessed her for helping me out. I lived there for a few months.

One night after Michael was released from jail, we slept in the shed behind his mother's house because we did not have a place to stay. The lady with whom I was staying had gone out with her male friend that night and I had been at my uncle's girlfriend's house late. When Michael and I returned, we couldn't get in so he took us to his mother's house. We couldn't go inside there either, so we went to the shed. The next morning we snuck out before his mother caught us. My son, Corey was old enough that he remembers that incident to this day. After being homeless for a while, I ended up getting another place and eventually losing it too. During the time I had the place, Michael stayed with me occasionally. I still had my children with me and was so broke that I would have to wash our clothes by hand in the bathtub. Additionally, we rode the bus everywhere we went. Corey had the bus route down so well that he would get our transfers before the driver would ask if we needed one. I would have Tashona on my hip, Corey by the hand and a diaper bag on the other arm. Furthermore, I even had to sell some of my food stamps at times in order to help pay the rent or a bill which meant we often ran out of food before the next month. Sometimes when we were out of food, I would pack the children up, walk to the grocery store, and steal food for them to eat.

Things had gotten pretty hard for me, nothing seemed to be working. I tried to go to school and had to quit because I did not have childcare for the kids. I had a physical fight with Jackie as I walked to the grocery store one day. Weeks later, Kav and Michael had a dispute that ended up in a shootout and Kav being hospitalized for a damaged eye. To top everything off, detectives began following me looking for information about Kav. One night I fearlessly walked through an alley, which was a shortcut to the store, and a detective stopped to interrogate me about Kav. He knew who I was and about our daughter and Kav's other female friends. He questioned me about things that Kav and his cousins had done while I neither confirmed nor denied anything. As I sat in the car with the detective, I realized that type of life style was not what I wanted. Obviously for the detective to know who I was, he had been watching me as well. He told me things to try and make me turn on Kav but one thing I learned during my time hanging in the streets was that the streets have an honor code and "snitches get stitches." The detective allowed me to leave after realizing that I wasn't going to provide him with any information.

Finally after my welfare was cut off, and I lost my place, I was totally unable to provide for my kids so I decided it was time to head back to Arkansas. Arkansas was always my safety net. There I knew if no one else loved me, my family did, especially my grandmother. I didn't return to live with my grandmother, but just knowing she was close by gave me comfort. I had reached the end of my rope as living in Kentucky had proven to be a big mistake. The love I thought I would find there and all of my big city dreams had faded away. This was the last time I ever lived in Louisville.

Luke 3:5 "Every valley shall be filled, and every mountain and hill shall be brought low, and the crooked shall be made straight, and the rough ways shall be made smooth..."

Fate

By December 1985, the kids and I were back in Arkansas. Although my mom allowed me to return back home, home was not where I really wanted to be. After having a taste of the big city, country life was no longer sufficient for me. My mom had a very successful beauty salon at this time and I was very proud of her. Most of my days were spent with my children and at my mom's salon.

It is amazing how one encounter can change a person's entire life. Accustomed to being back home, I was out one evening with my friend Tangila who was home visiting from the military. I was with her as she Christmas shopped. I was impressed when she pulled out her traveler's checks to pay for her purchases. Here I was on welfare and living with my mom, while she was doing so well for herself. I was happy for her because she was my friend, but I was also critical of how my life seemed to be going. She explained that she was a cook in the Army and suggested that I too enlist. We joked about it at first, but then I started thinking about it more seriously and figured it could be the answer for me and my children.

I knew Dewitt was not big enough to hold the dreams I held inside of me, therefore, a couple of days later I called Tangila and asked her to arrange a meeting with her recruiter and me. I also inquired about taking the test. Tangila was excited for me and I met her recruiter a few days before she had to return to her duty station which was in Savannah Georgia.

Shortly after, I took the test and scored so high that I had my choice of Military Occupation Specialties, or for civilians, job. I chose to go into foodservice although at this time I could barely boil water. As it turned out, my enlistment and MOS came with a $4000.00 bonus, which sounded as good to me as three million dollars. I would receive this bonus in addition to my regular pay after successfully completing all phases of training.

According to military regulations, in order for me to enlist, I had to sign custody of the children over to my mom and she would receive a dependent allowance each month for them. My mom was glad I was trying to do something positive with my life and happily agreed to take custody. New recruits received a booklet explaining what to expect as far as training so I began working out with Terry, Deborah's brother. He was a member of the National Guard and ran a couple miles each day. I started conditioning with him, running and doing pushups and sit ups every night. By the time November 1986 rolled around I was ready for basic training. Yeah right! What had I gotten into? I was soon to find out.

I Corinthians 2:14 "But the natural man received not the things of the Spirit of God: for they are foolishness unto him: neither can he know them, because they are spiritually discerned."

You're in the Army Now

*E*arly on I learned the meaning of a cattle truck. It was a truck that was actually used at one time to carry cattle. This is what I felt like as new recruits half sat and half stood on our way to the barracks on South Carolina's Tank Hill. The commercials didn't lie. In the military, we really did do more before 9:00 a.m. than most people did all day. As soon as we stepped off the cattle truck, drill sergeants were yelling and continued to yell every day for weeks as we did everything under the sun and ran four or five miles a day. I believe I cried every night in those first weeks of training.

I was generally a shy person, except around people I knew, so living in a barracks with thirty other girls with different backgrounds and personalities took some getting used to. Another thing that was weird to me was the fact that we were addressed only by our last names. I was no longer Twana, but Joyner. Last names made things simpler. Many of the new recruits were just out of high school, some were going from being weekend warriors to full time soldiers. Everyone had their own reasons. At twenty-two, I was one of the oldest persons in my platoon.

As we all prepared to leave, I could not help but feel remorseful. We had all become like family and I would miss all of them. Being from a small town, I had never had that many friends before. I kept my circle small and tight and liked it that way. But now, things were changing and I was beginning to feel more comfortable in my own skin. My shyness was subsiding and a newfound confidence was emerging, I felt like I really was being "all that I could be". Unbeknownst to me, God was grooming me to be a mouthpiece for Him.

After a small break, I headed to AIT, advanced individual training, which was another eight weeks. In AIT I learned my cooking skills. AIT was much more relaxed than basic training because after duty and on weekends, soldiers had free time on and off post. When the weeks ended, we received orders telling us where our permanent duty station would be. I was ordered to Ft. Benning Georgia. I was just happy to leave South Carolina. I had been there for Basic and AIT. All of my other friends had gone other places due to us having different MOS's. Upon graduation, finance gave me that $4000.00 bonus pay (minus taxes) and my regular pay. I had never had that much money at one time in my life! I held that little army issued black purse tightly and felt like a rich girl as I boarded my bus to Georgia. I was on my way to find out that peaches were not the only things sweet in Georgia. Here we go again.

Romans 7:14 "For we know that the law is spiritual,
but I am carnal, sold under sin."

The Meeting in the Break Room

As soon as I processed into my permanent duty station, I immediately converted my money into money orders and sent them to my mother for her to open me a checking account. I had never had a checking account before. I also sent a list of all of my immediate family members and put a dollar amount by each name. I wanted to share my wealth, so I told my mother to distribute it out to everyone. When I make my millions, I'll do the same thing. ☺

Brandon was a soldier in every sense of the word. He was smart, athletic and he loved his country. He had a great personality and everyone that came in contact with him liked him. Brandon spoiled me rotten. There was nothing he would not do for me if it was in his ability to do it. He had a great sense of humour and treated me like a lady.

Brandon and I had some rough times because he was somewhat of a cornball. It didn't take much before I was putting him out of my room and sending him to his. It was a co-ed building and we lived down the hall from each other. Though it was against the rules for males and females to be in the rooms of the opposite sex, it happened more often than not. Brandon practically lived in my room since my roommate was always in her boyfriend's room. About five months after meeting, Brandon proposed to me. Naturally, I was excited. I thought it was special that regardless of our ups and downs Brandon still wanted to marry me. He not only wanted to take on the responsibility of a wife, but father of my two children back home as well.

It wasn't long before the news of our engagement started spreading. Some people thought it was great, while others knew we had issues. One of those issues was Brandon's inability to keep my interest for long periods of time. It always seemed like we were only doing the same things—having sex, watching TV or going to the break room playing pool. I would break up with him and then we'd get back together again. I didn't realize how much my previous relationships had contributed to my commitment issues, but I figured once I got married those issues would fade. During one of the breakups, I started messing around. Brandon had found out I was talking to a guy in another unit and called off the engagement. Upset, one night I left his ring with the C.Q., charge of quarters, and went away for the weekend with the guy. When I returned to base, Brandon had decided he would talk to someone too. I felt I was justifiable by not doing my dirt in his face but felt he had disrespected me by having a girl come to the barracks and pick him up. Dirt was dirt, but I didn't see it that way.

One day I was in the dining facility and happened to look out to see Brandon and his little friend walking by. I went outside and confronted him. Before I knew it, I had jumped Brandon and started punching him. Talking about acting a fool! My friend Hawkins and some others came out of the facility and restrained me. I ran to my room enraged! Brandon had bought me a huge bear for Valentines that we named Donations because he was so expensive. Unfortunatley, Donations met his maker that day. Stuffing covered my entire room. Lizzie Bordon had nothing on me. Donations received 40 whacks and then some!I had been willing to dish it out, but had not been able to take it. I realized that either I wanted to have my cake and eat it too, or I had feelings for Brandon. The former would prove truer.

Romans 7:19 "For the good that I would I do not: but the evil which I would not, that I do."

Mental Breakdown

Over the next weeks as Brandon continued to date and my relationships fizzled, I went into depression. Another failed relationship was too much for me, so one day I decided that I would end it all and overdosed on pain pills. I just woke up one morning and decided I didn't want to live anymore. I felt that I had lost the only man who had or would ever love me. I was still searching for acceptance and love through people. When I had been given the very type of love I thought I had been searching for, I rejected it because I didn't recognize what it was. When I realized it was potentially gone, it was more than I could bear.

The day I overdosed, I didn't go downstairs to work and when my superiors came looking for me I was in the room crying hysterically. A sense of worthlessness had overtaken me and nothing mattered to me anymore. I was jealous that he had moved on and upset with myself for pushing him into her arms. The female sergeant that came to the room looking for me saw the pill bottle and called for an ambulance. I was rushed to the hospital and had my stomach pumped, which was a scary experience that almost cost me my military career and my life. After being released from the hospital, I had to meet with counselors and my sergeants to determine if I was mentally stable to remain in the military. I could not understand why I was not allowed to die when it appeared that I had nothing to live for. It's as if one day while lying in my bed thinking on that very thing that I saw the reflection of my children, Corey and Tashona and realized that they were the reason I went into the military in the first place and they were the reason I had to live. All the time I was trying to figure it out, God was already working it out. God still had plans for me there, so I was allowed to remain on active duty. Not even failing a drug test got me put out.

After the overdose, I began doing drugs again. Marijuana and speed were my drugs of choice. My friend Thomas had all types of connections and we often went off post and indulged, sometimes to the point that I could not even see straight. On one party binge, I had smoked a little too much not realizing that we were overdue to have a surprise urine test. Before I knew it, we were awakened early one morning to give urine samples. I was doomed. I had just smoked the day before which only added to all of the other drugs already in my system. A few days later, I was informed that I had failed. I would have to go before a full bird colonel and explain why I had failed the drug test. Of course I lied. I told him I had been at a party and must have inhaled it or some lame excuse like that. I know he did not believe me. Still he allowed me to keep my rank, and my money but I would have to perform 180 days of extra duty. Although that was a long time, it could have been a lot worse. Besides, I was able to do my extra duty right there in the dining facility where I already worked. It was only God's plan for me that allowed that to happen.

Brandon and I got back together in the midst of all of this and the engagement was back on. I don't know if he just felt sorry for me or what. One night as we lay in bed watching TV, we both vowed to stay faithful and to make our relationship work. You must under-

Mental Breakdown

stand that I had never really had a real relationship before. I did not truly know how to respond to a man that was so kind and faithful to me. I never knew that they really existed. It's amazing how easy it is to overlook something healthy and grab something unhealthy. I really believed my bad days were behind me. The very next day trouble walked through the dining facility door.

Psalm 146:9 "The Lord preserveth the strangers,
he relieveth the fatherless and widow:
but the way of the wicked he turneth upside down."

Love at First Sight

The day Specialist Nuniss walked into the dining facility is a day I will never forget. I was standing over by the sink and I saw him walk in the office with SFC Jones. They had paperwork so I knew he was about to become a member of our facility. I asked Thomas, my weed smoking buddy, if he knew who the new guy was. Thomas, crazy and nosey as he was, decided to find out by following the sergeant into the office. Thomas returned saying, "He's country as h_ _ _ and his name is Sol-a-thun, or Sal-athon Newni or something messed up like that." Thomas also explained that the new guy was from Florida and had just come from Korea. The new guy did not stay in the office long and soon left. However, the following day, he came back in the facility, only this time in civilian clothes. I had a cookie sheet in my hand and when he came through the door in a pair of overalls with no shirt underneath them, I looked at him and dropped the pan. He looked at me and smiled. That was it. From that day, I couldn't help looking at him. He was handsome and seemed charming.

We were introduced so I learned his first name was Solathian. At times I would catch him staring at me and he would catch me staring at him. It did not take long for him to learn that I was engaged since most of the talk around the facility those days was about my upcoming wedding in May. Over the course of time,

Solathian became close to another soldier in our facility named Singleton, whose nickname was "Ice." Solathian and I became great friends and Ice would become like my little brother. I found out that Solathian was still a young cat, about to turn twenty-one years old. I had just turned twenty-four in February. The age difference wasn't a big deal to me and from some of our conversations age was not a big issue to him either. In Korea, Solathian had dated a woman much older than I.

About a month before my wedding, Solathian and I had been flirting with each other a lot. We both knew I was about to get married but could not deny the attraction we had for each other. I began to look forward to going to work in order to see him and as the days drew closer, we talked about getting together before I made my walk down the aisle. The plan was for Solathian to rent a room at Super 8 Motel on a Saturday when Brandon had to work and I would meet him there. This motel was far from the base and we would make sure to hide our cars as best as possible. The Saturday arrived and I woke up feeling funny. I was cramping a little bit, but it wasn't time for "my friend." As I was getting dressed, however, the pains went away. I was very excited heading toward the motel. I arrived shortly after Solathian and after a brief hug we sat down on the bed and talked. One thing led to another, which ultimately led to us having sex. It had been a somewhat awkward experience because deep down I knew I was wrong.

Days later as I thought more about Solathian, I realized that there was something about him I really liked and it was different than anything I had experienced with anyone else. I was not foolish enough to believe that he had the same feelings for me, but I did believe that he realized that we had an undeniable chemistry. The problem was, however, I had a promise of marriage from someone who loved me. He and I did not get together in that way again and things between us had become awkward. Sometimes I felt that the sex had messed up a perfectly good friendship and had definitely put my upcoming marriage in jeopardy, but yet I could not get him out of my mind.

Finally after all the years of looking, Brandon actually wanted me to be his for the rest of our lives. Although I was only 24 years old at the time, it seemed as if I had already lived a lifetime. Alot had gone on in my young life and I was now about to embark on a lifetime commitment. My heart meant well but something deep in my gut was telling me I was making a huge mistake. Although my common sense was telling me that I should confess to Brandon that I had cheated, my selfishness convinced me that I was deserving of a man like Brandon and that the affair with Nuniss was over and would never happen again. Brandon made me feel special, unfortunately my lust for love–his love was not enough to keep me from compromising his heart.

Proverbs 11:21 "Though hand join in hand, the wicked shall not be unpunished: but the seed of the righteous shall be delivered"

It's My Wedding Day

May 15, 1988 was my wedding day and I was so excited. The past few weeks had been hectic, getting the bridesmaids dresses together, my dress, the cake, the reception center. We were having a church wedding believe it or not. I was glad for the great help provided by my friends Moore and Flowers. Also, the lady I hired for the decorations did a great job. My Uncle Carl, my little sister, Shenice, and my parents came from Arkansas and my stepfather would be giving me away.

As the music began to play, I grew nervous for the first time. I had my reservations because of the experience with Solathian. I loved Brandon, but did I love him enough to marry him? I had pondered these things only a week before and decided it was only my imagination – the same feelings I had for Brandon prior to meeting Solathian I still had. Besides, everything was already planned and I was not about to cancel everything and have us both looking like fools. Furthermore, Solathian had his own girlfriends and there was no guarantee that the two of us could ever be together. I felt "a husband in the hand was worth two in the bush."

Walking down the aisle, holding my dad's arm tight, the first person I saw was Solathian sitting by "Ice." They were both smiling with their crazy selves. Only the Lord knew what I was getting myself into.

The wedding went great and we went to the "Bicycle Club" for the reception. Brandon and I received so many gifts and had a great time celebrating with our friends and family. Brandon's mother and sister lived in Baltimore and his dad lived in North Carolina – none of them had been able to make it. After we left the Bicycle club, we gathered our gifts and headed to the apartment. Our friends planned on meeting us at a club later that night and Brandon and I planned to end our wedding night at a hotel. We all met at the club as planned and had a great time. My parents were there and I felt very proud to be a married woman. All the shame I felt at the hand of men in my past seemed to drift away as Brandon and I slow danced to a George Michael's song. I felt like Suge Avery from the movie, *The Color Purple,* "I's married now."

If only the night would have ended on a positive note, my feelings of insecurity may not have resurfaced so quickly. As it turned out, Brandon drank so much at the club he didn't have money for a decent hotel. Most of the hotels had been booked due to proms and graduations that were also going on that same night. Thus, we ended back up at the apartment with my parents in the next room. Talk about romantic.

Hebrews 13:4 "Marriage is honorable in all,
and the bed undefiled: but whoremongers and adulterers
God will judge"

~ *Chapter* IV ~

Here Went The Bride

*I*t seems like as soon as I walked down the aisle and Brandon and I were together on our wedding night, I knew I had made a mistake. Immediately, he began to get on my nerves. We had a really nice apartment, but we both were specialists so we really didn't make a lot of money to do extra stuff. Brandon was a sex maniac and sometimes I would pretend to be asleep in hopes that he would leave me alone. It did not work, however. I'd wait until he went to bed and was snoring. As soon as I thought I had success-fully gotten in bed without him waking, Brandon would roll over! I began to despise him touching me. I decided I wanted to make the marriage work, so I sucked it up and bared it. Things were not always bad. Brandon was very sweet and went out of his way to make me happy. I, however, was not used to being with a person that treated me the way he did, therefore I abused my privilege.

I was equally happy and sad when the company I was attached to announced we were going to Germany for winter training, Reforger '88. Something made me uneasy about leaving so soon after getting married. Somehow I felt things would not be the same when I returned. We had to prepare for months for the trip to Germany and things between Brandon and I were beginning to improve a bit, yet I was still unhappy. It definitely wasn't him – it was me. I had a good man in my life, a good career in the Army, yet there was still a void not allowing me to become totally fulfilled. I figured it must have been because my children were not with me. My mom had maintained custody from when I was in basic training and I sent her child support. I decided I would get them when I returned from Germany to fill the void that I had been trying to fill since childhood. I had a good husband, a career, everything except the picket fence. I would often imagine us all together doing things as a family. Part of me wanted it all and part of me was afraid of the responsibility.

I lay crying in my husband's arms the night before we left for Germany. He was not going because he was in a different service field. Instead, he was staying in Georgia. He reassured me everything would be okay and that he would take care of everything while I would be gone for forty-five days. Those forty-five days were simultaneously exciting and devastating in many ways.

I Timothy 3:11 "...Even so must their wives be grave, not slanderers, sober, faithful in all things"

ICH LEIBE DICH
(I Love You)

*M*an was it cold in Germany!!!! But it is one of the most beautiful places in the world. Being in Germany, I could understand why the Army slogan was "You can be all that you can be in the Army"!!! Many of us, no most of us, would have never gotten the chance to go overseas if it had not been for the Army. When our company arrived, things were very much unorganized. No one really knew where to go or what to do including our leaders. Everyone just kind of walked around out in the middle of nowhere until almost dark, then things started to come together.

Before it became too late, my company got our tents up and was finally settling in when Solathian and "Ice" came straggling in our tent. They were in a different company from the rest of us, but still worked in the same dining facility. Since we were cooks everyone wanted to be our friends when we were in the field but hated on us when we were back on base. There were now about 10 of us in one big tent, yet my eyes kept going to the side of the room with Solathian. I remember as we all began to prepare for bed, Solathian getting in his sleeping bag and taking his shirt off. He looked at me and I looked at him – we smiled at one another and in that moment we both had a flashback to the Super 8. There was something about him that I still could not deny, an attraction so deep that it really did not make sense to me. I had been in several relationships before, but none had made me feel the way I felt when I looked at him. I could already see that trouble was brewing.

Proverbs 24:8 "He that deviseth to do evil shall be called a mischievous person."

The Family

Being in Germany was one thing, being in Germany in the woods was another. We were up early, setting up tents, completing field exercises, and cooking. It was cold and the saying remained, "We did more before 9 a.m. than most people did all day." Solathian and Ice ended up being in our unit and it was very interesting. After duty we often spent time playing cards, talking, laughing a lot, taking baths behind sheets that we had set up, reading and just chilling out. We were like one big family. The field has a way of making people bond and become close, that is why so many military people stay in touch years after service.

Germany was indeed a beautiful country. Although we were in the field and away from the luxuries of life, we became a family. There were 2 female Sergeants that I became very close to Sgt. Oakley and Sgt. Grissett. They became the big sisters that I never had. We had a lot of good times and laughs, despite our living conditions.

Solathian and I had gotten to know each other pretty well also, we often talked and helped each other out with our work. The attraction I had for him was evident to others, especially, Sgt. Grissett. She knew we had a thing for each other and often teased me. She had her own thing going on also with a guy in the unit who was kind of sweet on her. Weeks passed and loneliness began to set in for many including myself. In order to pass the time, many people began to hook up and spend time with people that they normally would not have. Love was in the air, although no one was dolled up and looking cute. We quickly found out that in the dark it really did not matter.

Just as quickly as the field exercises began are as soon as they seemed to end. We had gotten so much accomplished in such a short amount of time and had fun in the process. One of the female soldiers that I knew from Fort Benning named Joyce, nicknamed Shorty because she was so short and petite, and I began to talk while we were out there. She was really cool and although we had spoken to each other back in Benning and lived next door to each other in the barracks, we had not previously gotten to know each other. I don't recall why I was looking for her, but when I went to her tent, it was like her barracks room. She had her own personal tent at this particular site and had it set up pretty comfortable with things that smelled good and snacks. We found out that we had a lot in common including a liking for two cooks that were best friends and currently working with the unit I was attached to. It was the beginning of a lasting friendship. We immediately began to devise a plan for when we would arrive at our final destination, tent city.

St. Matthew 26:41 "watch and pray that ye enter not into temptation: the spirit indeed is willing, but the flesh is weak."

The Opportunity

t the completion of the field exercises, each company packed and loaded on trucks headed for "Tent City," which would be our final destination before heading home. We would be there two more weeks. At this time we were able to have fun!!! We had such an interesting experience convoying to tent city. We actually got lost from the rest of the convoy. Sgt. Grissett had to use her personal money to buy gas and after driving around what seemed like forever. Luckily, we didn't enter enemy turf. We parked and tried to get some sleep until daylight. Thankfully, we began to hear voices and looked outside the truck. We had somehow managed to park right next to Tent City! We jumped off the truck and entered tents where people were having a good time playing cards and laughing and joking, unaware that we had been riding around in circles all night. We were so ecstatic to see everyone that we could not be mad at them. The assignment was officially over and the next day we would begin getting ready to tie up some loose ends for our return to the great U.S.A.

In Tent City, we could get passes to go off our post and eat restaurant food. It was like Heaven. It is here that my friend Shorty and I began to hang out. She and Ice liked each other, so we all devised a plan for her, Ice, Solathian and me to go off post and get a room. The plan was for the guys to ride in a cab together and we got our own cab. After a short pursuit from Shorty's ex who was also in tent city, we made it to the hotel safely. It was at this point that my feelings for Solathian went to another level. We sought opportunities to see each other as much as we could both on and off post. Although I was married, I felt a bond with him. Not only was I a married woman and a soldier, most of the members of Brandon's unit were there. It was risky, but to me it was worth all of the moments Solathian and I spent together. I must admit, sex played a big part in it.

When everyone boarded the plane to leave Germany, Solathian and I sat beside each other and talked what seems like the entire way. My heart began breaking as the pilot spoke over the intercom and said we were about to land in Georgia. Before we departed from the plane I scribbled three words on a piece of paper: Ich Leibe Dich. I learned them while in Germany and they meant "I love you". He looked at me and smiled. We left something in Germany that couldn't fit in either of our duffle bags, passion. For the first time in my life I was head over hills in love with someone. Reality reminded me of my husband at home, but my heart declared, "So what?" The plane landed. Solathian and I gave each other a quick peck on the cheek and departed from the plane. My life was never the same...

Proverbs 6:28, 29 "Can one go upon hot coals, and his feet not be burned? So he that goeth into his neighbors wife, shall not be innocent."

Home *Sweet* Home

etting off that plane and going into the hangar, the area where friends and loved ones waited was hard. I saw Brandon and my heart sank. He was cheesing hard and I tried to muster up a smile. Many of the returning soldiers had planned for a returning home celebration. I wanted to be a part of it, but those people were single. I could see in Brandon's eyes that he was anticipating a night of reuniting. Brandon waited for me to complete my reentry process then drove us home. As I entered the apartment, somewhat disappointed, I walked in to a table set for two–flowers, dimmed lights, candles waiting to be lit. It was so sweet that for a moment everything and everyone else faded and I appreciated my husband for his efforts.

Brandon gave me a bath and then we ate together, mostly in silence. My first night home, yet I was already wondering what the gang was doing and missing Germany. This was the first night I had spent in weeks without them and Solathian. For a moment I felt sad, then I realized that it was not just sadness. I had fallen in love. I was love sick and had acquired another soul tie. My life had become so complicated in a matter of weeks and I knew I had bitten off more than I could chew. If I only had known then, what I know now.

St Luke 5:31 "They that are whole need not a physician,
but they that are sick."

Creeping While He was Sleeping

Finally I went back to work and things went back to normal. Well as normal as they could be. Solathian and I were trying constantly to figure out a way to get together. It had been almost two weeks since we had been alone and I was missing him. I was emotionally cheating on my husband although at the time I did not know that it was possible to cheat without having sex. If your emotions are attached to a person other than the one you are married to, it is emotional infidelity. My husband ended up being put on night shift which opened up a door that allowed me more time on my hands that I could handle. I began meeting with Solathian wherever, whenever we could. We would go somewhere and have sex, or talk or both. Neither of us liked the fact that we had to sneak, but we both knew it was necessary. Additionally, I knew that Solathian was a good-looking guy and other girls were interested in dating him. It was beginning to make me jealous seeing him talk to them. He quickly reminded me that I was married and he didn't like having to sneak around either. Although he made his true feelings about our situation known to me, he also made it clear that he was not ready to stop seeing me and still desired to be with me. It was at that point that I realized how he truly felt about me. So many other opportunities were in his face on a daily basis and although I personally did not believe that he was totally committed to me and me only—I did believe that he had love for me.

Shorty and I were now best friends and she and "Ice" had gotten pretty close. They both knew Solathian and I were still messing around and often had to be our messengers. One night one of my dining facility sergeants had a get together at his house and our crew all went over. We all drank and got drunk. Since the sergeant's house wasn't far from mine, I told Solathian to stop by my house on his way back to the base which he did. My husband was due to get off work within 2 hours and I had to go pick him up. I drove on base drunk with an E&J brandy bottle in my lap. When Brandon saw me, he was furious that I had come on base in that condition. He immediately got in the driver's seat. I knew I had to tell him that Solathian was there so I reluctantly told him Solathian was at our house because we had all gotten drunk down the street at SFC Peters house and I didn't want him to get a ticket driving on the military base. He looked at me bewildered considering that I had driven on base drunk. At first Brandon was disturbed by the news, but I made it clear to him if he made Solathian leave then I was leaving too because he was being selfish. Drunks are so foolishly bold! Being the sensible person that he was, Brandon agreed to let him stay. We went home and went to bed. He wanted sex, I didn't. I rolled over to go to sleep still holding a bottle of E&J Brandy.

The next day was Saturday and my husband had duty. Solathian and I did not. When Solathian awakened he could not believe he had stayed the night in my home. He was nervous, but I told him my husband had left already for work. I called to ensure that Brandon indeed was at work and then I invited Solathian into my bed, the king size bed – he reluctantly came. After sex he left and I was left there alone, trying to figure out how I could have the man I had such a connection with and hating myself for making such a big mistake by marrying Brandon. I was becoming so bold with my adultery that it was scaring me. I never should have gotten married. I should not have been cheating on my husband and I should not have been involving Solathian in such a dangerous situation. Both of our military careers could have been destroyed because of our fraternization. I was totally messed up – still searching for love although I had a husband that loved me. I did not understand my self and was often in states of depression. I turned back to drugs and had started drinking more than I ever had before. My life was spiraling out of control and not only was it affecting me, it was affecting others. I was selfish and uncaring about anything that did not concern me being happy. Although we had always been careful with our sneaking around, I knew that what was done in the dark would one day have to come to the light. I was in a bad situation that would only get worse.

Psalms 24:17 "The troubles of my heart are enlarged:
O bring thou me out of my distresses"

More Drama

The bad thing about lying and cheating is eventually you forget what the lies are and what the truth is. Becoming careless with cheating, inevitably gets you caught. Solathian had written me a letter and signed it with an alias, Slatewood. He had also given me a picture. I had the picture in my wallet and the letter in my purse. Normally Brandon never went in my purse, but fate would have it that one particular night he decided to look for a cigarette in my purse after I had refused him sex. The next thing I remember was the door swinging back and Brandon yelling, "I know this "isn't true"! It scared me, so I jumped up and asked why he was yelling. Then I saw the letter in his hand.

I dashed toward the door but he grabbed me. He dragged me into the living room and demanded that I call this "Slatewood" person at the barracks. I lied saying it was very early in the morning and the C.Q. couldn't leave his post to get him. Brandon then had me call Shorty to try to get her to go get Slatewood. Shorty and I were so close that Brandon knew if anything was going on and someone knew about it, it was her. Shorty and I had good non-communication skills and she figured out something was wrong, so from her end of the phone she asked me questions while I answered "yes and no". She figured out that under no circumstances should she go and get Slatewood a.k.a. Solathian. I hung up and told

Brandon that she refused because he lived in another barracks.

Although Solathian was off the hook, I wasn't. Brandon mentally abused me until sunrise. It was question after question. Yelling and screaming. Pulling and tugging. I wanted to go to bed and he wouldn't allow me. I felt like one of the Taliban. I still didn't tell him the truth about the author of the letter. Brandon saw the picture of Solathian as well, but I told him Solathian had given me that picture a while back, before we had gotten married. Since Solathian had used an alias on the letter, Brandon had no clue that the picture and letter came from the same person. I felt like a spider caught up in my own sticky web. Well everyone knows how the story of the spider caught up in the sticky web ends right?

Proverbs 12:4 "A virtuous woman is a crown to her husband: but she that maketh ashamed is as rottenness in his bones"

What A Tangled Web We Weave...

The web of deception, there are so many twist and turns that it is hard to know when or where to go at times. I refused to stop messing around with Solathian although I knew I needed to do so. It was like being addicted to crack cocaine – it was calling me. Brandon was a good husband, but now I didn't want him to be my husband. I wanted him to go away. That didn't happen. What did happen one morning when the alarm clock went off was me saying, "Nuniss, turn the clock off." Brandon looked at me and I made up some lie about Nuniss being the one in charge of waking us all up when we were in the field.

~ · ~

I was on a steady downhill fall and I couldn't catch myself. Before I knew it Brandon and I were arguing with each other every day. I couldn't stand it any longer so while he was at work one day, I packed up everything I could fit in my car. I sat outside in the parking lot in front of our apartment complex for what seemed liked hours. I was trying to get up the nerve to drive off. I knew that once I drove off, things were about to change and I did not know if I was prepared for the aftershock. I put the car in reverse and drove to the army base and found my friend Pate. She agreed to let me secretly stay in her room in the barracks. Brandon waited for me to pick him up that day, but I never showed. Needless to say, he began asking around for me. He knew I was messing around, but at that point he did not know with whom. I was trying to work, hide out, see Solathian, and keep my sanity. Man, was it hard!!!! Then it happened. Haphazardly, Brandon was in the wrong place for me, the right place for him, at the wrong time for me and the right time for him when he heard Solathian's best friend "Ice" refer to him as "Slatewood". What are the odds?? Exactly! I was told that Brandon asked who Slatewood was and he told him Nuniss. Ice was unaware of the mayhem that happened with the photo and letter – he was totally in the dark about the entire situation.

The devil doesn't play fair. He is a deceiver. He gets you out there – then he sets you up for the fall.

Proverbs 5:19 "The way of the wicked is as darkness: They know not at what they stumble."

~ Chapter V ~

The Fall

Wow, didn't it hurt!!! Although I was in an emotional battle, I found myself feeling sorry for Brandon. I didn't want to hurt him, but that was all I ended up doing. I came to realize that I was never in love with Brandon to the degree of marriage. I had never been married before. I simply was twenty-four years old and felt like it was time, not realizing that at twenty-four I was just beginning to find out who I was as an adult. All the warning signs had been there but I had ignored them. My soul mate had walked into the door and I didn't have the spiritual discernment to know.

Brandon eventually found me and confronted me about my whereabouts. I explained to him that I had enough and was not planning on returning to our apartment. I tried to talk to him reasonably but of course that did not work. He explained how I inconvenienced him by not having a ride to and from work and how I was his wife and could not just up and leave and think it was okay. He also questioned if the reason I left had anything to do with Nuniss A.K.A. Slatewood. Imagine my surprise when he said that. Lies really do catch up with you. The skeletons in my closets were shaking and I did not know where the bones would end up falling. I told him I was sorry for the inconvenience and did not know how we would get him to work but I needed time to get myself together and no my leaving had nothing to do with Nuniss. As soon as the words left my lips, I knew it was a lie. After hours of sitting in the car and hours of me saying the same thing over and over again, Brandon finally tired himself out and left it alone, temporarily. I didn't realize that his leaving it alone was really a set up to catch me in the act, or as close to the act as possible. Brandon found ways to get to work and when he could not, I would go outside and the car would be gone. Since I was on base he felt I did not need it and I could understand where he was coming from but my selfishness did not allow me to see things that way at the time.

I was still living in the Delta Company barracks with my girl Pate, when on a Friday night like many others, Brandon had come over to harass me. I could tell he had been drinking so I tried to keep our argument brief. Reluctantly he left after about 30 minutes of slightly slurring his words and grabbing on me as I tried to walk away. The rumor was that he had begun drinking and possibly smoking on a regular basis. A lot of people on the base knew that I left Brandon and thought I was a terrible person because of it. Many suspected and others knew that I was involved with Solathian, including the First Sergeant of the company. I was preparing to go to the NCO club that night with my girls. Solathian would be there also. Luckily Brandon had not taken the car so I drove over and parked in front of Charlie Company barracks in order to pick Shorty up but she was nowhere in sight. Usually she watched for me to pull up in the barracks parking lot. Little did I know that while I was sitting outside, there was a full fledge fight going on in the barracks and Shorty had ringside seats. Solathian and Brandon were throwing down!! Leon and Muhammad didn't have anything on these two...

Proverbs 15:13 "a merry heart maketh a cheerful countenance: but by sorrow of the heart the spirit is broken"

The Throw Down Caused
By The Lowdown

According to Shorty, apparently Brandon happened to be in the building meeting up with one of his friends to also go out. While Brandon was in the hallway waiting and conversing with some other friends, Solathian walked in to pick up Ice from Shorty's room as they were going out also. A spirit of boldness came over Brandon, since by now he was sure that Solathian was the one with whom I had been messing around. Brandon's boys being in the hallway only fueled his anger as I can only assume he felt like a punk that was being further disrespected by Solathian entering in his company's barracks.

Brandon apparently charged down the hallway screaming profanities at Solathian before he could even make it to Shorty's door. He began confronting him about "his wife" and punched Solathian. From that point Shorty and Ice heard the commotion and looked out. Brandon and Solathian were duking it out. Solathian was short and muscular and Brandon was tall and of medium build. Regardless of size, according to sources, Solathian gave Brandon a beat down! Now I don't know that for sure, but that's what I heard. After the fight was broken up, Brandon made threats about him not being at the club or Solathian would get it again. Of course, Solathian took him up on it.

During this time, I was still sitting downstairs in the Charlie Company parking lot across from Solathian's barracks. I saw Solathian and Ice going up the stairs. Solathian was walking as if he was tired and with his shirt off. I wondered what the heck was going on, but had no clue that he and Brandon had just fought. I don't remember how Shorty and I made contact but somehow we did. She gave me the blow by blow as we headed to the club......

Job 5:6, 7 "Although affliction cometh not forth of the dust,
neither doth trouble spring out of the ground,
yet man is born unto trouble, as the sparks fly upward."

Da Club

We all arrived at the club as Shorty continued to fill me in on the details. I felt sad because I never wanted them to fight each other. The truth of the matter was I loved Solathian, but felt guilty for hurting Brandon because he really was a good man. Brandon wasn't the type of man to cheat and he was good for me. It broke my heart that either of them was hurt. They both were at the club and someone informed us that Brandon had a gun. I knew that wasn't true. No matter how angry he was, Brandon would not do anything that crazy. He was just trying to intimidate Solathian who was now upset with me.

I was a nervous wreck! I was ducking behind chairs and dodging around the room like a crazy person. The NCO club was packed that night as always and I did not want Solathian to be so mad at me that he would talk to someone right there in my face like he had done before. I was also trying to keep my eyes on Brandon. He was walking around in the very expensive leather jacket I had purchased him for Christmas with one hand tucked on the inside. I knew that he was not crazy enough to actually do anything like shooting anyone, but I was not sure if the word had gotten out about the earlier fight or whether any of our commanders had gotten wind. I was also afraid that they may run up on each other again in the club.

I tried talking to Solathian, but he told me he wasn't going through the bull anymore; it was over between us because I was married. At this point I knew I had a choice to make and it wasn't going to be an easy one. Finally I had found the man of my dreams, yet I was destroying another man's life. Life really is about choices, sometimes we get it right and many times we fail, but ultimately we have to choose. I was trying to hold on to something that was good for me and at the same time I wanted to keep what was feeling good to me. As I sat at the table in the club alone, drinking and crying, I tried to figure out why my life was so messed up, I mean, I just wanted to be happy. As I sat there trying to get my dressed up, messed up self together, I decided to find Shorty so we could get out of there. As I searched for her, I saw Brandon and Solathian still walking around with their respective crews. I finally found Shorty and as we left the club, a revelation hit me–the song with the lyrics "trying to love two-show ain't easy to do "was absolutely right.

Psalm 127:1 "Except the Lord build the house, they labour in vain that build it: except the Lord keep the city, the watchman waketh but in vain."

Stolen Moments

I don't recall exactly how Solathian and I began talking again, but we were just like magnets. The only difference was now he had met someone and was going out more during the week and hanging out more with Ice. He was trying to move on with his life, but still we would find those times to steal away. When it was time to part ways, reality would hit and I would realize that I was still married. I began to get jealous of Solathian seeing other girls more and more often, although he kept denying it to me. As a woman you just know. I couldn't blame him much, regardless it hurt and I found myself crying a lot. The fact that we worked in the same dining facility also did not help matters. This meant we saw each other every day whether we wanted to or not. When things were good between us it was good seeing him but when things were bad, we ignored each other as if we did not know who the other was. Lately things had been pretty bad.

Mostly everything I owned was in the trunk of my car and at times Brandon would still come and steal the car just to aggravate me. I tried to stay out of his path, but every now and then he would see if we could just talk. Every time we did, it ended with him getting angry. His entire character had changed. I had created a monster. Love had turned him bitter and I knew I was to blame. He truly loved me and I had been selfish not to let him know that the

112

feelings were not mutual.

When I was with Solathian everything felt so natural and right. Sometimes we would both cry when we had to part ways. I knew he loved me and I loved him. What I did not know was if it was true love or only an illusion like so many times before. I had a bird in the hand but wanted the one in the bush. I knew that I could not have my cake and eat it too although at times I wish I could have. I knew that along the way, in my quest for love there would be casualties. In this instance, I did not want it to be me. I made up my mind – it was time to end the drama.

Galatians 6:3 "For if a man think himself to be something, when he is nothing, he deceiveth himself"

No More Drama?

*E*ventually I spoke to an attorney about getting a divorce. Brandon and I had just gotten married in May 1988 and by January 1989 I was filing for divorce. We had already been separated for a couple months. By this time I had made up my mind that I could not stay married whether Solathian and I got together or not. My lawyer was cold hearted and had the papers delivered to Brandon on Valentine's Day. Naturally Brandon called me very upset. He had no idea that I was filing for divorce and was perturbed. Apparently some of his friends were at the apartment with him when the papers were delivered. I did not plan it – it just turned out that way.

Though I felt badly, at the same time I was relieved that this drama was about to be over in my life. However, by this time, Solathian was really out there playing the field and I was still in love with him. He wasn't real excited when I told him I had filed for divorce because I had made promises to file before and had not followed through with it. He thought I was playing games and began to seek comfort in other single girls. I was afraid he would fall in love and I didn't know if I could handle what I had dished out.

I Corinthians 7:10 "And unto the married I command, yet not I, but the Lord, Let not the wife depart from her husband: But if depart, let her remain unmarried, or be reconciled to her husband: and let not the husband put away his wife."

Mission: Possible

The following months were miserable for me as I was trying to be a "soldier" while at the same time keep up with Solathian and lose Brandon. I was finding out that all three were full time jobs. Solathian and I became more distant and Brandon was trying to pull our marriage back together. One day our Sergeant announced that our unit would be going to the field. All of my field gear was still at the apartment which meant I would have to either sneak in or face Brandon in order to get it. I chose to sneak in. I knew he worked night duty so sneaking in should have been pretty easy to do. Just my luck, I found out from my sources he was off that particular night and to top things off, earlier that day he had stolen the car. I called it stealing, but everyone else called it a husband using his wife's car. I beat myself up every time I thought about the fact that I let him invest a few hundred dollars into that car.

Shorty and I got with someone who agreed to take us to the apartment to get my things that night. We devised a plan to meet at around 21:00 hrs. (9:00 p.m.) and hope Brandon was gone. We got together as planned and went to the apartment. The car was gone. I had them park their car on the other side of the complex because Brandon would recognize their car if he saw it. A hill separated the two sides, so I ran across it like I was about to take over Bunker Hill or something. I then made a mad dash to the front door of the apartment. We had agreed that if I wasn't back in 5 minutes, Shorty would send in the reinforcement.

Once inside, I ran through the house collecting my things. I couldn't help but stop for a minute and look because the apartment looked just like I had left it. Everything was in place. I chose to leave him everything, although I had purchased most of the things. My freedom had meant more than any material things. I got my military gear and headed out. As I was about to run across the street to cross the hill, I looked to my left and saw headlights that looked familiar. The headlights on my car had a funny kind of glimmer to them and it was them. I didn't stop. I kept running right in front of the car and hit that hill. I looked back. Brandon saw that it was me and sped up and tried to make it to the other side before I did. The only problem for him was that he would have to drive all the way around. Luckily, Shorty and our other accomplice had also seen him drive through and had the car ready and waiting. Shorty threw open the door and I dived inside it.

As soon as I got in, Brandon made it around and was trying to stop us by blowing his horn. We rolled right out of the apartment complex and sped away. As I looked back, I saw those little glimmering lights turn right to head back to the apartments. We were laughing, adrenaline pumping, smoking and joking. It was just like a scene from *Charlie's Angels*. I laughed on the outside, but inside I felt terrible because I had not wanted to resort to such behavior. My heart was leading me to do all the wrong things for what I thought were all the right reasons.

I Corinthians 8:2 "And if any man think that he knoweth any thing, he knoweth nothing yet as he ought to know."

Korea Bound

Since my relationship with both Brandon and Solathian were so entangled I decided I would just leave both of them alone and take a tour to Korea. Solathian had previously told me about the shopping and how a single woman could go there never really having to spend any money because of all the soldiers that were more than willing to do so. I talked to Shorty and she helped me with the process of getting orders to Korea. Within a few months I was informed that there would be a slot becoming available in the summer and I was on the list for it. I also began taking classes at the community college to keep my mind off things.

Solathian and I still saw each other occasionally and finally Brandon had taken a break from harassing me. I began to notice that Solathian seemed to be drinking a lot more and staying gone all night away from the barracks. When I visited his room one night all of his stereo equipment was gone. He explained how he had pawned it, but I knew that was a lie. The rumor was he was staying nights with some civilian girl he had met at the NCO Club. Of course he denied it.

Weeks passed and I finally received my orders for Korea – they were for the end of May 1989. During a night of passion I told Solathian that I received orders and was leaving for Korea the end of May. He didn't believe me at first, but when I showed him the orders that required me to get a Top Secret security clearance, he said he would try to go with me. I didn't believe him, but the very next day he started working on getting an assignment. Within weeks he had orders also. It appeared that everything was going to be okay. Solathian and I would go to Korea together, although we would not be in the same unit or even the same part of Korea, it seemed like we would get to start all over. My divorce was due to be final in May as well. It was perfect timing and then the news.

Matthew 10:26 "...for there is nothing covered, that shall not be revealed: and hid that shall not be known."

My News, His News

I had been feeling sluggish lately, but I also knew I had been under a lot of stress so I did not think much about it at first. However, since the sluggishness persisted, I decided to go to sick call and find out what may have been wrong. I walked out of sick call a changed woman. The Army was not going to let me go to Korea pregnant!

I wasn't upset about being pregnant. I was upset because I couldn't leave Georgia. Since Brandon and I had not been intimate in so long, I knew without a doubt as I checked my calendar that I was pregnant by Solathian. We had discussed having a child together at one point. I even went as far as having my IUD, (inter-uterine device), removed per Solathian's request. I believed in my heart that one day we would be together and would have children together. However, I did not expect to get pregnant so quickly.

I didn't tell Solathian at first because I was unsure about how he would take the news. A few days later I mustered up the nerve. I mentioned abortion and he cursed me out. I truly did not want to have an abortion, but I wanted to see where Solathian's mind was in regards to the pregnancy. He wasn't happy and he wasn't sad – he was just surprised. I told him I would not tell my superior officers that I was pregnant and go to Korea anyway. He immediately disapproved of the idea explaining the various vaccines that I would have to take since Korea was a third world country. Thus, he was unsure of the medical impacts on the baby and was afraid the baby would be mentally or physically damaged. He conversely threatened to tell my superiors if I tried to go while pregnant though ultimately he was a little disappointed that he would have to still go to Korea. The only reason he signed up to begin with was to be with me. This would be his second tour in less than two years.

A week later the two of us were together in one of our secret spots and Solathian surprised me with the question he asked. He asked if I would marry him when my divorce became final. I was shocked but extremely excited that he wanted me to be his wife. Immediately I said, "Yes!" I felt like finally I would be with the man I loved. When I returned to work the following day at the dining facility, I disclosed to my sergeant that I was pregnant. Although it had taken a couple of months to get orders to go to Korea, it did not take very long for them to be revoked. Since I was pregnant, I would be able to get off-post housing, therefore, I planned to get my children so we could all finally live together. Corey was now seven and Tashona was five.

The clock was ticking. I was waiting on my divorce to become final, working on getting my children to Georgia and coming to grips with being pregnant again after so many years. Time was drawing nearer for Solathian's departure when he confessed to me. We were on the way to main post when he confessed that during a time when we were not together he had briefly dated and slept with a girl named Brandy who had recently told him that she too was pregnant. Her child was due in December and mine was due in November. Brandy and I were due one month apart! I almost flipped my wig! I went off! I told him that he could be with her because there was no way I was going to marry him. I was sick about it. I wouldn't speak to him although he kept coming to my house. I was literally sick! My heart was broken once again and I knew that my dirt had caught up with me. I was in love, but this situation was not at all new to me – it was déjà vu actually. I was in the same situation as I had been when I got pregnant at 17–multiple babies, one daddy.

Proverbs 26:11 "As a dog returneth to his vomit, so a fool returneth to his folly."

The Day Before

After countless attempts to salvage our relationship, I stuck to my guns and remained furious with Solathian. It was the ultimate offense in my opinion. He kept saying it was not serious between them, but I suspected otherwise. I felt totally betrayed so he would use the "you were still married" card on me. I still wasn't buying it. He was down to a couple of days before leaving. I kept pondering about how what had seemed like a perfect situation had turned horrible so quickly. Still, one thing I knew for sure was that I was still in love with Solathian and there was no way to deny it. After some deep heart to hearts and lots of crying on my part, I finally agreed to marry him still.

My divorce papers were only a week and a half old when I walked in the downtown Columbus, Georgia courthouse and married Solathian. We only shared one night together as husband and wife before he left for his hometown of Pensacola, Florida where he was scheduled to depart from a day later for Korea. His mother later told me that while at the airport she saw the wedding ring on his left hand and asked if he had gotten married. He confirmed and when she asked him why, he told her he didn't know. The last bell had rung, the fat lady had sung and the time had come for me to begin reaping what I had sown.

St. Matthew 13:4 "And when he sowed, some seeds fell by the wayside, and the fowls came and devoured them up..."

123

A New Addition

During the summer, and shortly after Solathian's departure, Corey and Tashona came to live with me. My sister also came to stay with me for the summer and baby sat them until they started to school in the fall. It was a long hot summer and money was scarce. One day my sister said she looked in the refrigerator and didn't see any food and all of a sudden she said everything went black. She had mentally blacked out! It was funny the way she described it, but I could relate. I was getting paid once a month and it was not enough to maintain my car payment, insurance, food, phone and clothing bills. I was only a specialist in the Army at the time and was thankful that I didn't have a mortgage and utilities. Otherwise, I would have been living back in the barracks. However, I did eventually get food and my sister stopped seeing blackness.

After the summer ended, the children started school and I began preparing for the birth of the little Nuniss child. I must admit that my life had changed dramatically and it seemed that it changed overnight. Not only did I now have my children on a permanent basis but I was pregnant and my husband was thousands of miles away.

Halloween came and the children wanted to go trick or treating. Although I was 8 1/2 months pregnant I agreed to take them but told them I would not get out of the car. I did not expect to see so many people in the neighborhood we had driven to. There were ghosts and goblins and all kinds of other creatures running from

124

building to building. Cars were bumper to bumper as other parents had the same idea that I did-children get out, go to a few homes, come back to the car-none of the children were doing that however, including mine. I lost track of them and had to drive around the block and come back. I was scared for a moment but soon saw the two of them beaming with a lantern full of goodies.

I had spoken to my mom a few weeks earlier and she had agreed to come to Georgia and stay with me to help out with the new baby for awhile.

November finally arrived and exactly on the due date Ms. Katecia was born. Solathian had picked out the names. He had given me two to choose from and I chose Katecia. Earlier that morning I had felt pains and my mom, who had come to be with me, started timing my contractions. They were exactly five minutes apart. They weren't hard pains, so I thought it may have been a false alarm but we headed to the hospital anyway. When we made it into the parking lot and began walking to the hospital a contraction stopped me in my tracks. A few more feet and another one hit. My mom and I were laughing because of the way the contractions kept stopping me. I tried to make it through the huge waiting area before another one hit, but as soon as I got midway one struck. Everyone looked as if I was about to have the baby right there!

My mother thought it was hilarious. When I finally got upstairs to the maternity ward and they checked me, I was already dilated eight centimeters. Full dilation is ten. It was about 10:55 a.m. Katecia was born at 11:05 a.m. on November 7, 1989.

Galatians 4:23 "But he who was of the bondwoman was born after the flesh, but he of the freewoman was by promise."

125

~ Chapter VI ~

Be Careful What You Ask For: Round 1

lot happened while Solathian was away in Korea. For the first time, I had Corey and Tashona in a home with me that was also safe for them. The new baby kept all of us on our toes because she was so smart. Every day she was learning something new. Although Solathian and I were married, what was his was his and what was mine was mine. Financially, he was not really able to be a support for me. Distance was also proving to cause problems in our relationship. He was miserable being in Korea and I was miserable without him. The problem was neither of us knew how to handle the stress which in turn caused our marriage to suffer. I contemplated a brief affair while he was gone due to the stresses of our letters, but I did not want to complicate my love life any further. Thus, I declined a fellow soldier's advances and dealt as best as I could with the loneliness. I was beginning to feel that the distance between Solathian and I was more than either of us could bear. The other baby he was expecting was born a month after Katecia and I knew in my heart that Solathian kept in touch with her mother as much as he did with me. To further complicate things, Solathian's mom wasn't very optimistic about our marriage and reiterated the fact that he did not know why he married me. Naturally that did not help matters between Solathian and I. I was anxious for Solathian to return in order for me to see for myself what I was dealing with.

I should have been more careful about what I asked for. Everything I craved I got but I was not prepared for the consequences that came along with satisfying my sweet tooth.

May 1990 Solathian arrived from Korea with goodies for everyone. All of the children had Nike, Gucci and Fila, even the baby. He had purses and shoes and jogging suits for me, as well as jogging suits for the children with their names on them. He also had stuff for his other daughter. He had already shipped her mother her things, which I wasn't supposed to know about.

It must have been the second day of Solathian being home when things began to go completely awry, and I received the first phone call from Brandy, the baby's mother. I answered the phone, pre-caller I.D. or cell phone era, and all I could hear was crying. When we were able to clearly communicate, Brandy asked to speak with Solathian because the baby needed to go to the doctor. I immediately got upset because the baby was five months old and I wondered who was taking her to the doctor before he had returned to the states. I also was uncertain of how she had gotten my phone number. Dumbfounded, I gave Solathian the phone. When he got off and said he needed to take the baby to the doctor, I knew then the interaction between he and Brandy was about to be a problem.

Over the next year the baby momma drama was in full force. Solathian and I were at odds all the time because I suspected he was doing more than seeing the baby when he went over to Brandy's house. Because he told his mother and Brandy that I had something against her baby, the baby wasn't allowed over to our house. Making matters worse, Solathian's mother was often involved in her children's affairs so our business was not entirely "our" business.

The person I was then was a far cry from the person I am today – consequently, she and I weren't the best of friends. I, the wife, was the bad guy and Brandy, the baby mamma, was the angel. I knew better, but I really didn't care what any of them thought, including Solathian.

I tried to figure out how in such a short time things between Solathian and I had changed so much. One night when he was out, I began meddling around in his bag that held a lot of his army papers and inside there was a large bag of letters. Some of them were letters I had written to him while he was away and some were letters Brandy had written. Additionally, there were pictures of her scantily clad and pictures of the baby. As I sat there and began to read her letters, I saw why things were different. These were love letters and the entire time he was in Korea they had been writing and making plans to get together when he returned home. It felt as if a knife had been driven in my chest as I read each letter. When he returned home that night, the letters were left out for him to see. He couldn't say anything but I had plenty to say and none of it was nice. The seeds I had planted years ago were growing up like weeds in a flower bed. It was only the beginning.

Proverbs 11:27 "He that diligently seeketh good procureth favour: but he that seeketh mischief, it shall come unto him"

The Deception

he Persian Gulf War began and since I had planned to stay in the military, it appeared that both Solathian and I would have to go to the Persian Gulf. After all the trio drama between Solathian, Brandon and myself, I switched units and posts. That way I would not have to face Brandon or any of the other people in my old unit. Although I changed units, Brandon still found me and called my new unit one day to talk with me. I worked in the office so I happened to answer the phone when he called. I answered the phone as usual, "Specialist Nuniss speaking." The voice on the other end asked, "Twana is that you?" It was Brandon, He was shocked because I had gotten remarried and I was shocked because he had called! Needless to say, we had a very interesting conversation.

It was undetermined if Solathian and I would be stationed together, but I still was not enthusiastic about going to the Persian Gulf. I wasn't afraid of the war. I didn't want to have to send the children off and possibly separate them for an indefinite period of time. By the grace of God, my new commander agreed to let me honorable discharge from the military since my enlistment period was about to end. Solathian, however, would still have to go.

The time quickly came for Solathian's departure and they would be deploying from Ft. Stewart, which was in Savannah, Georgia. My friend Debra and I decided to drive down to Savannah to see our husbands off to war. We had hotel rooms on post and the guys were allowed to stay with us each night. The days went by pretty quickly and before long we were heading back home. Two months later I found out that I was pregnant again.

Although Solathian and I had had some pretty good two or three days before he left, we still had major issues. I didn't trust him as far as I could see him and divorce had been mentioned by both us more than once. Katecia was only seven months old and I wasn't ready for another baby. Solathian's mother and I had somewhat called a truce and began to communicate more often. She often kept Katecia and Kari for weeks or even months at a time. She had become one of my confidantes, or so I thought. Therefore, after finding out I was pregnant, I called her one night and told her the news. She asked me if I thought having another baby was a good idea considering that things were not going so well between Solathian and me. She went on to tell me that he had plans to possibly divorce me when he returned. Though Solathian's mother never directly told me to have an abortion or give the baby up for adoption, I could tell she wasn't too keen on the idea of me having another child by her son.

I was close to three months when I made the decision to have an abortion. I thought, cried about, and analyzed my situation. Looking at my other three children and my marriage failing, I realized I would be overwhelmed being left to take care of not only the three of them but a new baby as well. I felt that it would be too much for me to handle considering the uncertainty of my marriage, so I called around and got the name of a clinic that was located in Atlanta and scheduled an appointment. A friend and fellow soldier drove me to the abortion clinic in Atlanta.

Arriving at the clinic, there were protestors lining the streets on both sides. It was just like I had seen in movies. The protestors had signs with pictures of babies that had been aborted and were chanting "Baby Killers!" It was so bad that the clinic had people outside to lead patients to an underground parking deck. When we parked, I began to cry. My friend just sat there silent as I got myself together before entering the clinic. There were young women, older women and some that did not look like they were old enough to be considered a woman. Looking around at all of the girls, I questioned the integrity of the clinic as I noticed that some of them appeared to be too young to be making such a grown-up decision. Before I had time to get the nerve to back out, a nurse approached me with a sign-in-sheet and a lot of papers to fill out. I remember sitting there looking at all the other girls and feeling so empty inside. Shortly after completing the paperwork, a nurse called my name and after giving my friend an "I don't know if this is what I should do" look, I was led to another room in the back of the clinic. The hallway was very long and every step felt like I had suddenly placed weights around my ankles. Once there, I was given a gown and taken into a room for testing to determine how far along I was.

After the tests were completed I was led into a second room. The room was very bright and all of the equipment looked old. It was like a doctor's office from the 1960's. I was told to lie back on the examining table and to relax. A different nurse came in with a needle in her hand and gave me an injection that she explained would put me to sleep in order for them to perform the procedure. I was afraid and I remember tears beginning to stream down my face. The nurse had a stern face, not at all compassionate like the nurses you see at regular hospitals. I could only imagine how many babies she had saw killed and how many tears she had seen running down the faces of their killers. As I began dozing off, I only remember seeing the nurse's face and hearing her say count backwards from ten. All I recall saying was "10."

I don't know how much time passed before I awakened but when I did, a different nurse smiled at me and handed me my clothes. I could not control my tears as I got dressed. Driving by the protestors, I hid my face and cried. As a matter of fact, I believe that I cried all the way back to Columbus.

The following day I called Solathian's mom and told her the news. She said it may have been best and promised not to tell Solathian because he was already under a great deal of stress being in a war zone. About 2 months passed and I was just beginning to get back to normal after dealing with a bout of depression and regret. I still had not told anyone about the abortion, not even my family. I was too ashamed about what I had done. My family was very close and no one I knew of had ever had an abortion. Everyone had their babies and dealt with the consequences of their choices. I often wondered if the baby was a boy or a girl and what I would have named him or her. I even asked God to forgive me but I did not believe that he would since one of the Ten Commandments was "thou shalt not kill". I felt so badly about killing my baby but there was no way to undo what had been done. I knew without a doubt that I was surely destined for Hell. To make matters worse, it was around this time that I received the letter from Solathian. I had received others, but none like this one. In the letter he proclaimed how he hated me for killing his baby, and how he wanted me to move out of the government quarters where the children and I were living. I was civilian now so the military housing was now in his name. I could not believe that his mother had told him and deceived me like that. I had always been nice to her and could not understand why she disliked me so much. When I called her to ask her about it she said it had slipped. How does something like that slip? Anyway, she proceeded to tell me that he told her to come and clear out the quarters. I told her she was welcome to come and get her son's things, but I wasn't going anywhere. When a person shows you who they are–believe them. The truce was over.

Micah 7:6 "For the son dishonored the father, the daughter riseth up against her mother, the daughter riseth up against her mother, the daughter in law against her mother in law, a man's enemies are the men of his own house."

Be Careful What You Ask For: Round 2

*O*ne year passed by quickly and before I knew it Solathian was heading back home. I was grateful that God had kept him safe. He eventually forgave me for what I had done or so he said and our letters, though short, were civil. He had called to let me know when he would be arriving back in Georgia. He asked me to be at the hangar where they would be arriving and to bring Katecia. I had begun working as an assistant manager at Godfather's Pizza at night and could not afford a babysitter so my teenage cousin, Angela, was living with me in order to babysit. On the day Solathian was to arrive, his mother called and inquired if I was going to meet Solathian and I gave her an indirect response – at this point I didn't trust her anymore. She was going to be coming from Florida to meet him as well. That night I packed up all the children and Angela and I headed to the hangar to greet the soldiers. There were so many people there that it was hard getting up close to see the guys as they were deplaning. Angie and I saw an open spot right up front and ran to get it before anyone else could, laughing all the while. When we got to the spot, I turned to my left and there stood Solathian's mom, stepdad, brother, Kari and Kari's mother. We all saw one another at the same time. I held Katecia in my arms and his mom greeted me while reaching for Katecia. I did not want to, but I let her hold Katecia for a few minutes.

My cousin and I looked at each other, for we both had figured out why his mom wanted to know whether I would be there to greet Solathian. It was the first time Brandy, Kari's mom, and I had come face to face. I held my ground and stayed right where I was. I wanted everyone else to feel as uncomfortable as they had made me. We finally saw Solathian come off the plane. He scanned the crowd and then he locked in on us. I could have bought him for a penny as he saw ALL of us standing there. I can only imagine what he was thinking. Soon after the soldiers were officially released everyone went to greet their soldiers. As we all approached Solathian he tried to stay cool by speaking to everyone and taking both his daughters, one in each arm. After a couple of awkward minutes, I took Katecia and began to leave with the other children and my cousin. I figured it was Solathian who had planned for his other family to be there and I had no energy or time for drama. However, as I walked off, Solathian called my name. He wanted me to wait because he was going home with us. He parted from his family and we left together and of course we argued all the way home and after we got home. Only a few short hours later, he left claiming that he was going to see his mom before they left for Florida. It turns out that he stayed out all night and supposedly went to Atlanta. If he went to Atlanta, I was sure he did not go alone. Brandy had sisters in that area. Naturally I was hot as a $5.00 pistol. I had been up all night again, reading letters of her love for him and I could only imagine what he was telling her. It's almost as if he kept the letters just for me to see. He wasn't man enough at the time to just end either our marriage or his affair with Brandy. He needed to keep us both for some reason. My theory was to avoid having to pay me more child support, His theory may be different.

Often, I contemplated just killing Solathian in his sleep, but thought better since I didn't want to go to prison. I did however purchase a gun from a guy off the street and made sure that Solathian knew that I had it. I always kept it hidden, hoping that I would not have to use it. Needless to say, he began to be more discreet. Still I knew when he said he was going here, that he was probably going there. When he said he would be home in a minute, it would be in an hour or two hours.

I constantly wondered how I had ended up with another fool. It wasn't long before it dawned on me. I had asked for it. This was the man that a few years back I did not mind giving up my marriage, my dignity, my integrity or pride for. Well now I had him. But it wasn't him, not the "him" I had fallen in love with. Situations, people and circumstances had caused us both to become different and I had grown tired. Only time would tell if what we had would be able to stand the tests and trials that were ahead.

John 16:33 "...In the world ye shall tribulation: but be of good cheer, I have overcome the world."

The Other (Other) Woman

For months Solathian's behavior continued to be out of control. He continuously drank and went out to the clubs. He was hardly ever at home. I was still working as an assistant manager at Godfather's Pizza in Columbus and usually worked every weekend so we hardly saw each other. I thought about filing for divorce but didn't have the money to do it. He was paying me child support although we were living in the same house. Each month when he paid child support for his other daughter, he would write me a check also. I was tired of him and decided I needed a break. Thus, I took some time off from work and went to Arkansas for two weeks.

When I returned, I noticed the sliding back door was not working properly. Since we hardly used it, I wondered why. When I went upstairs to put my things away, I sat down on the bed a minute and saw a long piece of black hair on the bedspread. It did not take long for me to put two and two together. Before I had left for Arkansas there was a young girl around 19 that had moved in a few houses down with her sister and brother-in-law. She was mixed race with long black hair. Not only could I do math, my ears were as keen as a deer during hunting season. Although our bedroom was on the opposite side from the parking area, I always heard the car door close when Solathian came home on Saturday nights. On one particular night, I heard the door close, but it took him a long time to get to the front door. I thought he may have passed out or something, so I went and peeped out of the den window. When I looked out, I saw him standing and talking to the young girl. It was around three in the morning and no one was sitting out as they sometimes did on Saturday nights. As I looked out the window, it appeared that they may have been arguing. I didn't know they knew each other well enough to be arguing. His younger brother from Florida had visited us before I left for Arkansas and talked to the girl during his visit so I thought he was the one that liked her, but it appeared that big brother had taken over. By the time Solathian made it upstairs, I could no longer contain myself and demanded to know who he was talking to outside. He identified the girl. Of course I demanded to know why. He pathetically claimed that the conversation was about his brother. I didn't buy it but before I could ask any more questions he was in the bed snoring. The next day I confronted him about the hair, the sliding door and the previous night. I told him about my suspicions of him sneaking her in the backdoor at night while I was gone so our nosey next door neighbor wouldn't see her coming into the house. Of course he denied it, but my intuition told me I was right. Years later he confessed to me that what I had suspected was true.

Proverbs 18:8 "The words of a talebearer are as wounds, and they go down into the innermost parts of the belly."

More Orders To Deploy

*T*alk about reaping. I was a mental wreck. I was still in love, yet struggling to hold on most days. For the life of me, I didn't understand why I could not walk away from this marriage. My answer was getting closer than I imagined. Solathian had not been home from the gulf a complete year when he got orders to deploy to Germany. The quick turnaround on his orders was odd, but God does things in mysterious ways.

From the beginning of our courthouse wedding, Solathian and I were married on paper but not in spirit. I had basically given up on our marriage and was only waiting for him to file for divorce. He always said he was going to but never did. I felt it was because of our daughter and the fact that he knew I was vengeful at that time and may or may not let him see her. Initially when he received his orders, "we" were going to Germany – the entire family. After a disagreement we had, somehow it ended up as "he" was going to Germany. I was done, finished, hanging up the towel – that was the last straw. The fat lady was singing once again.

I was tired of his selfishness. I was tired of his cheating and lying and I was tired of being married to him. Whoever wanted him could have him as far as I was concerned. That included the little chocolate girl in the photo lying on his cot while he was in the Persian Gulf. She even had the nerve to call the house asking to speak to him proclaiming that Sgt. Nuniss had been counseling her. I was sure he had been indeed. The foxhole on a hot desert night probably made a great "counseling" room. I warned her not to call anymore and that she better get her counseling from him at the base.

I finally packed up everything the children owned in terms of clothes, loaded my car, and with my children headed to Arkansas. I had gotten the courage to leave at last. I must admit that it hurt as I pulled my car out of that parking lot but I knew in my heart if I did not leave him, I would probably kill him. That was how much anger, hurt and disappointment I had inside of me. I wasn't doing drugs during this time, mainly because I didn't know anyone else who was and who could supply them. All of my old buddies, including Shorty were already in Germany or elsewhere. I had slowed down from my barracks days when Shorty and I were mixing gin and juice in my car on the way to the club and it was as if Solathian was just getting started. I wanted some type of drug to ease the pain, something stronger than marijuana, but God did not allow me to find it. I realized that our relationship was finally over. Solathian had been my prince charming, my soul mate, my one true love, but it had also been two years and my happily ever after was nowhere in sight. I left Georgia heartbroken and empty inside. I cried for hours as my children slept in the backseat. I thought of doing something drastic like driving someplace where no one knew us and starting a new life but as soon as the thought came into my head—I was crossing the Arkansas State Line.

Proverbs 26:27 "Whoso diggeth a pit shall fall therein: and he that rolleth a stone, it will return upon him."

The Duck House

I returned to Arkansas as always, this time with three children. After staying with my mother and dad for a while, my Aunt Linda agreed to let me stay with her and her two daughters in Pine Bluff, Arkansas. It was only a forty-five minute drive from Dewitt. Aunt Linda was a nurse and worked two jobs. We named the house she lived in the "duck house" because it was white and had three or four yellow ducks painted on the outside. It sat close to the end of the street and a Taco Bell was on the corner across the street. Taco Bell and their ninety-nine cent chilitos became our best friends. My aunt was hardly ever home because she worked hard to provide for her children.

I liked Pine Bluff because it was urban and much like what I had grown accustomed. The girls and I would have so much fun each day recording videos of us singing and dancing. Each night we had a video to show my aunt who thought they were pretty good. I wasn't sure where things were heading for Solathian and me so I applied for food stamps and he sent me child support.

One night while hanging out with my aunt I met a guy. He was immediately attracted to me, but I wasn't to him at first. After talking for a while, I found him to be charming and funny and gave him my number. He lived in Little Rock but hung out in Pine bluff a lot. Either I would drive the forty-five minutes to see him or he would come see me. I knew that our relationship would not evolve into anything serious, but I enjoyed his company. Solathian was scheduled to go to Germany in December of 1991 and it was already October. We would talk on occasion but nothing to the effect of me going with him to Germany. Consequently, I began to look for a job and a place to stay. I had come to the conclusion that my marriage to Solathian was over. I was smoking weed again often with a male friend of the family. I was trying to medicate my broken heart, but not even the weed was working anymore. On one occasion, I rode with the friend to someone's home that he was taking weed to. As we all sat in the car to sample the new product, I quickly realized that this was not ordinary weed. It had a strange smell and it got me higher than I had ever been. I asked my friend what it was and he said that it was regular weed but had something extra on it. I don't know what it was for certain, but what I do know is that the very next day I woke up wanting more. I was craving it so badly. I tried to find the friend's number but could not find it. All day the thought of that high stayed on my mind. God knew the plans he had for me and they were ones of good and not evil and he knew the expected end.

A few weeks before Thanksgiving I received the call that put God's plan in motion.

Psalm 34:18 "The Lord is nigh unto them that are of a broken heart, and saveth such as be of a contrite spirit."

It Ain't Over til It's Over

A few weeks before Thanksgiving Solathian called. After asking about Katecia and the other children, he asked me if I was going with him to Germany. I must admit I was very shocked to say the least. I asked him if he was sure he wanted me to go and he gave a sarcastic, "I wouldn't have asked you if I hadn't." He went on to tell me that we were on his orders to accompany him and I would have to get the children's paperwork and passports. He didn't go into a lot of detail but he did tell me he would be going to Florida before coming to see us in Arkansas. I was excited and nervous because I wasn't positive if I even would be able to go to Germany.

Weeks prior I and two others had gotten caught stealing jeans and other items in the mall. It wasn't a felony – nevertheless, we had gotten caught and I had a court date. Although one of the girls took the blame, we were all together and I did have a pair of jeans in my possession. I did not understand why she took the blame at the time (thank you again) or why Solathian had a change of heart. Later on I realized why—I had an appointment with destiny.

Jeremiah 11:23 "O Lord, I know that the way of man is not in himself, it is not in man that walketh to direct his steps."

~ *Chapter* VII ~

It's Off! It's On!

Solathian arrived in Arkansas about two weeks before Thanksgiving prior to leaving for Germany. We were to get the children situated with clothes and our paperwork for Germany. I must admit I was glad to see him at first but soon I realized that he was not so happy to be there.

Thanksgiving came and my mother had her yearly birthday party at "Gene's Place" back home in Dewitt. Linda, Solathian and I went to help her celebrate and my grandmother kept all of the grand-children. Everyone looked forward to my mom's parties because she spared no expense and went out of her way to make sure everyone had plenty to eat and a good time. My mom's hair salon was still doing well and she and my stepfather loved entertaining their family and friends during the holidays. I loved seeing my parents so happy. The party was a success and Solathian and I had a blast. He ended up all over the home-made video that was being shot of the event.

Still, things between us were definitely strained. Once again, one evening while going through his things I found letters that had been written to him from another female and all heck broke loose! What was up with all these letters? I was tired of finding letters. But like the scripture tells us, if you seek, ye shall find! As angry as I was, I could not understand for the life of me why he would even bring the letters unless he wanted me to find them. It didn't matter the reason. I vowed to not go to Germany. For him that was fine. He claimed he was glad that I wasn't going. He packed his things and left earlier than planned on his way back to Florida. I thought to myself, *Si Renada! Arevaderche! Good Bye! And good riddance!* I was glad he was gone!

About a week later, right before it was time for him to deploy for Germany, he called me and asked me to go again. He didn't apologize for his behavior or offer an explanation about the letters – he just wanted to know if I was still going to Germany. At first I was reluctant, but I knew I didn't really want to stay in Arkansas and I didn't have a place of my own. Ultimately I agreed to go. I figured I would at least get to see Germany and if I had to come back, so be it.

Solathian and I were holding on but neither of us knew why. We were unaware that things were happening in the spiritual realm that we had no control over in the natural realm. It would be only months before we would both come to any realization. We had nothing to do with our connection to one another. The plan for our lives was greater than either of us could ever be. I went to court the following week for the jean incident and had to pay restitution. Luckily, it would not interfere with me going to Germany. Solathian left in December, the children and I were not scheduled to leave until February once he got housing and everything set up. I had no idea that my life was about to take on a whole new meaning and would never nor could ever, be the same.

Jeremiah 29:11 "For I know the thoughts that I think toward you, saith the Lord, thoughts of peace, and not of evil, to give you an expected end."

A Return to The Scene of The Crime

The children and I arrived in Heidelberg, Germany in February 1992, a week or so before my birthday. It was such a beautiful country. Solathian met us at the airport in Frankfurt which was about a two hour drive to Heidelberg. We talked all the way and he informed me of where we would be living and a little bit about the culture. It had been a very long flight and we were all exhausted. On the plane it had seemed that every time I woke up, they were serving breakfast. They actually had been because we kept changing time zones. A boring movie was played on the big screen and the plane was the largest I had ever seen. The row we sat on had enough seats for me and my three children and a couple other people. Although there was a movie playing, I was more entertained by the family that sat across from us. The family was an older woman with six children, mainly boys who sniffed their food each time before they would eat it. I found it odd and couldn't wait until another meal was served. They went back and forth sampling each other's food. I watched them off and on throughout the flight, but for the most part my children and I slept.

After arriving in Germany, I could not help but think back to the last time we had been in Germany together as Solathian drove. It had been Reforger '88. Here we were four years later and so many things had changed. We had been secret lovers then, now we were husband and wife with three children. Things obviously were not the same as in 1988. Back then we were trying to find ways to get together and now we were trying to find ways to keep from separating. Just as he had been puzzled years ago about why he married me, I was puzzled about why we were staying married. There was a reason I had to be in Germany at that particular time but I had no idea what that reason was.

Romans 9:16 "So then it is not of him that willeth, nor of him that runneth, but of God that sheweth mercy."

Patrick Henry Village

The military housing we lived in was called Patrick Henry Village. It was right outside Heidelberg and not at all on base as the housing was in the States. In the beginning I had to memorize the building number of our home since all the buildings looked the same, just the way the military liked it. We lived in an apartment of four bedroom and two baths without having to pay electric, gas, or water bills – all we had was the telephone bill. Talk about living the life! With the financial opportunities, I could understand why some families had been in the military for years. After living in Germany for years as active military personnel, one friend and her husband had bought a brand new car and all new furniture before they left for the United States. They had been able to save a lot of money while there. I quickly found that saving money wasn't hard to do since there weren't really a lot of extra-curricular or entertaining things to do over there aside from going to clubs, the bowling alley, or the movies. I loved our neighborhood. From our living room window was the view of a huge historic castle. Additionally, I liked the fact that the children's school was right there in the neighborhood and so was Katecia's daycare.

It wasn't long before I got a job at the commissary as a stocker and was making pretty good money for the times, especially since we didn't have any bills except telephone, car payment and insurance. Solathian had been promoted to Staff Sergeant, but he was still pretty stingy with his money. He had begun to regularly go to the clubs again once we got settled in and it was okay with me because my friend, Shorty, who was now married, had been stationed in Germany for a little over a year and had found out where we were. Shorty was like my little sister and I was excited that I wasn't in Germany alone. When we finally met up, it was just like the scene from *The Color Purple* where Nettie and Celie were reunited! I couldn't believe it. Shorty was my road dog, my ace, and my partner in crime! Shorty and I were back together again!

Proverbs 17:17 "A friend loveth at all times, and a brother is born for adversity."

The Reunion

*H*ere I was with Solathian and the kids in Heidelberg, Germany and my friend Shorty, who was now married, was living only about thirty minutes away in Karlsruhe. On top of that, our other military friend, Debra, from our stationing in Georgia, and her husband were also neighbors to Shorty in Karlsruhe. The first time we all got together was at Shorty's house and we had a big barbeque like old times in Georgia. We had a blast! Shorty had been living in Germany for a little while and knew her way around pretty well, so we eventually began clubbing again. Because I worked nights at the commissary, I wasn't off every weekend but the weekends I was off, I was usually hanging out over Shorty's house or we would go out. Solathian would head out in one direction and I would go the opposite. I don't recall one time that we went out together the entire time we were living in Germany. Before long, Solathian had a wide array of friends and because Shorty is such a people person, she introduced me to lots of her friends that she and I would hang out with.

While working at the commissary, I began doing drugs again. There were a couple guys there that smoked "hashish." I didn't quite understand what it was when they tried telling me about it, but it was black and kind of wet and it was smoked as a mix with tobacco from a cigarette. I liked it because unlike weed, it didn't leave my eyes all red or a strong smell on my clothes. From the first time I smoked it, I was hooked. Hashish had become my new love and my new drug of choice. I was afraid to try any of that other foreign stuff. I remember one night my friend Greg had come to meet Shorty and me at the club in Karlsruhe. He had some really good stuff with him that he wanted me to try out. We sat in his car and as soon as we began smoking I could tell it was different. I took maybe four puffs and I was so high I could not see straight. I asked him if it was laced and he said no. It was pure hashish. When I went back into the club, I immediately began wondering how I was going to get home. I had a thirty minute drive back to Heidelberg and I did not know how I was going to make it because I was so high. When I sat down by Shorty, she looked at me and immediately knew I was messed up. Even though we were in the dark she could still see my eyes dancing. I went out on the dance floor and must have danced ten songs in a row until I was able to come down to a level of high that I could maintain. I think of those days now and realize that all those times I got on the Autobahn high and drunk, God encamped angels around my car and kept me for his purpose.

II Timothy 2:13 "If we believe not, yet he abideth faithful: he cannot deny himself."

The Countdown

By November 1992, I had gotten another job working for the Department of Defense as a payroll technician. It was more money and I enjoyed the job but I was still getting high and going out pretty often with my friends. Before I got the payroll job I would sometimes pretend to go to the night job at the commissary and actually do a superman change in the car and head to the club instead. Clubbing was my new way of escaping from the unhappy home life with Solathian. We lived together as husband and wife but we did not interact like husband and wife. By this time, I was not the same woman that previously sat in the house and cried everyday wondering where her husband was. A monster had been created and her nickname was Tee. It was now a different ball game and I was just as much to blame for the tension in our marriage as he was. I figured, if you can't beat 'em join 'em.

Our daughter Katecia celebrated her third birthday on Nov. 7, 1992 and Solathian's parents flew all the way to Germany to be there for it. They loved Ms. Katecia. Since another lady at my job was having a party for her son whose birthday was a few days after Katecia's, we decided to combine the parties. It was an awesome birthday party! Lots of children and adults flooded our apartment. The adults sipped on mixed drinks and the children had every kind of party food known to man. Today my daughter still has the tape from the party and trips out on how spoiled she was.

A couple days after the party we got the most disturbing phone call from Florida. Solathian's youngest brother called crying and asking to speak to his mom. "Little Mamma," Solathian's great-grandmother had died. Naturally, everyone was torn up about it, Solathian even more so because he, his mom and grandmothers were all very close. My heart went out to him and the family.

The next day he began calling and making arrangements to go home with his mom and step dad. None of the plans included Corey and I. Tashona was back in the States at the time with my mom. The Army would have given him advances so all of us could go, but of course Solathian thought only of the money he would have to pay back. I also believe he just really wanted to be with his maternal family and to have the freedom to see his other daughter and female friends while he was home.

Eventually plans were arranged and he was taking Katecia with him. I was thankful that he would be gone for thirty whole days. I talked to Shorty and began to celebrate. I would have the house to myself and could do what I wanted for thirty whole days. I immediately began to think of getting together with this guy, Sgt. Simmons, whom I had met at the club in Karlsruhe. He was very handsome, single and nice. We had been trying to get together for a while but had not been able. I knew this would be my chance. Unbeknownst to me the countdown had started and the announcer was counting down, "5.4.3.2.1."

Proverbs 16:9 "A man's heart deviseth his way:
but the Lord directeth his steps."

My First Encounter

*J*ust nights before Solathian and his family were scheduled to leave for the States we had a pretty emotional night and Solathian did a lot of crying. He was deeply saddened because of the death of his great-grandmother and I could understand his pain. That night as we went to bed in silence, I wrapped my arm around him to offer him comfort which he accepted. I must have dozed off pretty suddenly, but when I awoke I was lying on my back unable to move my body.

I lied in bed and felt some kind of presence over me. I tried to scream but nothing came out. I felt whatever it was lie on top of me. It was as if someone had laid a soft blanket, yet heavy, over me. My eyes were open and I could see, but I could not see anything placed on top of me. I don't know how much time passed, but all of a sudden I felt a smile cross my face and "the blanket" lift itself off of me. I immediately rose up straight and grabbed hold to Solathian, who was sleeping soundly with his back towards me. I held on tight – he didn't budge. All of a sudden fear engulfed me and I started thinking that it was "Little Mamma's" spirit that had visited me. That made me afraid although I had felt peaceful when "the blanket" had rested on me. I did not understand it.

After "the blanket" experience, I did not want Solathian to leave Corey and me in the scary house alone for thirty days. I was terrified and tried explaining things to Solathian but of course he did not understand. I had not had any more experiences so I wasn't quite as afraid by the time the family left for the states.

I immediately got on the phone with Shorty and began making plans for the upcoming weekend. Everything was set with Simmons and we were scheduled to meet up at the NCO Club in Karlsruhe Saturday night. After feeling so rejected by Solathian, I thought I was deserving of a good little fling. After all, I was sure Solathian was seeing someone else. He was gone too often and loved the club too much. He and I had crept around on my ex-husband so I knew he knew how to do it and I hadn't forgotten either – so it was on. Old habits seemed to die hard.

Saturday night couldn't come fast enough. It was just like the first time I had met Simmons at the NCO club in Karlsruhe, he appeared really gentlemanly and looked so adorably good. Our first attempts of being together had been interrupted by an ex-girlfriend of his. One night while in Karlsruhe at a barbeque, Shorty and I decided to go to a talent show taking place later that night. Solathian already had taken the children home and Shorty was going to take me home later that night. Simmons was there and we managed to get away and go to his room in the barracks. Well, just as things were about to get heated up, we heard a female at the door telling him to open the door. Of course he didn't respond. After a few minutes she left and we picked up where we had left off.

We were still clothed but working toward getting unclothed. All of a sudden we heard something on the side of the building. Simmons lived on the second floor and this girl had somehow climbed up the building and was trying to get her leg through his window! He looked at me and said, "I ought to push her off." Instead he went over in disbelief and assisted her before she fell and killed her crazy self. She did not address me directly but demanded that he explain who I was. To make a long story short, he got rid of her and drove me to Heidelberg. I had him to let me out around the corner and he promised me that he would make it up to me and asked if he could have a rain check. I went in my house, laughing to myself at the female and slightly disappointed that our night had been inter-rupted. Finally the time had come to cash in on the rain check. If loving Simmons was wrong, I didn't want to be right. How wrong I was, another soul tie.

James 4:17 "Therefore to him that knoweth to do good and doeth it not, to him it is sin."

My Second Encounter

*S*aturday night finally came and once again I was in Karlsruhe with my home girl Shorty for another great night at the NCO club. The club was jumping and we were already having a good time when Simmons walked in. I saw him but for the first time I saw things in a different light. I began to feel uncomfortable with the thought that I was possibly about to cheat on my husband. I also began to reflect on my "blanket" encounter. It was a weird feeling, but I soon shrugged it off and got back in the moment.

Simmons came over and spoke to me and we slow danced. In the midst of the dance he asked me if he could take me home. Of course I agreed. I could not wait until the night ended. As the DJ announced the last song of the night, I saw Simmons head my way. He asked if I was ready to go. I left Shorty and promised to call her the next day. Simmons and I left the club headed to Heidelberg. I was somewhat nervous but at the same time excited.

Simmons and I made small talk on the way to my home and once there finally had sex. There were not any fireworks or anything special about it. It was just sex. This time I did not just feel empty inside, it was deeper than that, for the first time, my soul felt dirty. Early the next morning Simmons left and believe it or not, I was glad. Something about me was different. I looked the same on the outside but internally felt different. I sat in bed that day and became curious about God.

A few days later while sitting in my living room, I noticed my husband's Bible inside the China cabinet. It was a Bible that once had belonged to "Little Mamma." Although he never read it, it was very special to him. I retrieved it and when I opened it up, all of the words looked like Greek to me. An eerie feeling came over me and I quickly replaced the Bible in the cabinet. The fear was back and I started sleeping with the lights on again. If Corey was outside playing, I was outside with him. I peeped down the hall before coming or going down it and if the floor creaked, I freaked!

I had been talking to Shorty, devising new plans, but my heart just wasn't into hanging out. The weekend came and I did not go anywhere. I decided to stay home with Corey Saturday night and he and I watched movies. He didn't know the reason I was keeping him so close was because I was afraid. He thought we were bonding. Well, we were bonding, but just not for the reasons he thought. I could not let him know I was afraid or else he would have used that against me. Corey was a prankster — I didn't want to take any chances of him jumping from around a corner to purposely scare me and it end by me taking him out! Later that Saturday night, I had my second encounter with what I would later find out was the Holy Spirit.

Romans 13:12 "The night is far spent, the day is at hand: let us therefore cast off the works of darkness, and let us put on the armour of light."

~ *Chapter* VIII ~

Let's Go To Chuurch!

On the second Saturday night after Solathian had left, I was lying across my bed with the lights on. Corey was already asleep in bed. All of a sudden I began to feel like someone was standing in the room watching me. I didn't see anyone, but I could feel the presence of someone or something in the room. Initially I was scared, but then the feeling left. I fell asleep and when I woke up it was midnight and I could hear a voice telling me to go to church. It was not an audible voice, yet I heard it. I fell to sleep again and I awoke to the same thing at 1:00 a.m. Every hour on the hour I would wake up and hear the same thing in my head. At 7:00 a.m. when I awakened I heard Corey getting up.

I asked Corey if he knew where there was a church. He did because he had gone with our upstairs neighbors once. The church he spoke of was not on post so I asked him if he remembered how to get there and he did. I told him to get dressed because we were going to church. Astonished, he stared at me. Up to this point, I had never taken my children to church nor had I been to church myself in years. All I had was clothes for work and the club but nothing that looked "churchy." I told Corey to find the best looking outfit he had because of course, the children did not have clothes for church either. I looked in my closet and decided the skirts I had were too short for church so I would have to wear a nice pair of slacks and a blouse. I hoped they would not throw me out of the church for having on pants. I had once heard you are supposed to go to the church "just as you are" so that's exactly what I was going to have to do.

Corey did not miss a twist or a turn. He knew exactly how to get there and we arrived at the church just as the service was beginning. It felt strange to be there. I remembered how my mother and step-father would take us every now and then when I was younger. At one point they even had gotten pretty consistent and both became ushers. Still, I had not been in a church other than for funerals since I was a little girl. The last time I had been in a church was for my great grandfather, Will Perkin's funeral back in 1984. "Grandpa Will," as we called him, was born on July 7th, 1898 and had died on December 7th, 1984. He was my Grandmother Cora's father and she was his only child.

Although short lived, my first introduction to God came through my parents as it should be. My brothers and I mainly wrote notes throughout the service and waited for the woman named Mrs. Mae Foster to "get happy" and scream out.(Forgive us, we didn't know any better). When we were there I sang in a choir that sang the same song every Sunday, "He's Able", but I never knew what the pastor was talking about. Our consistency in going to church was short lived, but my first introduction to church came through my parents at St. John Baptist Church in Ethel Arkansas.

This church, however, was different in many ways from the little Baptist one we attended in Arkansas. The music was different– the atmosphere was different – and everyone appeared so nice and happy to be there. Only after the praise and worship part of the service had ended and the "Bishop," had stepped to the podium to speak, did I know why they all had smiles on their faces. Bishop spoke with such authority as he delivered his message. I still remember that his message was about how bodies are temples and when we put things in them that do not belong we are polluting our temples. As he spoke, I thought about how I had been polluting my temple by smoking and drinking.

By the time Bishop was finished preaching, I was totally convicted. I remember leaving the church in a daze. The service had been awesome and I had felt so good while I was there. I was glad the voice in my head had told me to go to church. When I got home, I looked at the pack of cigarettes I had and I thought of the Bishop's message. I immediately tore them up. I didn't want to pollute my temple any longer.

> **I Corinthians 6:19:** "What? Know ye not that your body is the
> temple of the Holy Ghost which is in you,
> which ye have of God, and ye are not your own?"

The Transformation

The work week began the next day and I felt very good, changed even. Going to church had made me feel wonderful and caused me to look at life differently. It had only been one day but I still had not smoked or thought about smoking another cigarette. I could not believe that just by asking God to take the desire to smoke away that he would do it and do it so quickly. I did not really know how to pray at this time, but I remember hearing Bishop say, "Just ask God to take those desires away and He will do it." I had done just that. Friday came and Shorty called. We had not talked all week. I told her about church and how I had quit smoking, which she didn't believe but I told her she would see. Shorty was trying to make plans for Saturday night, but I had not really thought about it because I had been so consumed thinking about what I had learned at church. Nonchalantly, I told her we could go to the club and I would meet her there. Saturday came and I met Shorty at the club. The club was pretty boring and not packed that night as some of the units were in the field. Consequently, we left the club early and I went home.

I actually was beginning to miss Solathian. It had been two weeks since he had been gone and it would be another two weeks before he would return. I went home, got in bed and fell right asleep. I woke up early the next morning, which was Sunday. I thought about visiting the church again but I felt bad after having gone to the club the night before. Corey wanted to know if we were going to church that morning and I told him we were not. I could tell he was disappointed because he had really enjoyed himself the previous Sunday. However, as I sat on the couch thinking, the voice in my head returned telling me to go anyway. It seemed the longer I sat there, the stronger the urge got, so I told Corey to get dressed and we went.

We made it to church just on time again and sat at the back of the church. The praise and worship began and as the choir began to sing, I began to cry. I didn't know why I was crying but I sat there and cried and cried. There were other people waving their hands in the air and crying also. Some were dancing with the music, others were on their knees praying. I had never experienced anything like it before in my life. There was such a peace in the building with everyone worshipping God in their own way. I felt ashamed for sitting there crying, but after witnessing all that was going on, the shame dissipated. Corey moved close to me and put his hand on my shoulder. I noticed he had a tissue in his hand and he began to wipe my face.

When Bishop began preaching, it was just like the Sunday before. The message he preached pertained to me once again and I cried through most of it but left there feeling refreshed. My week was filled with feelings that I had never experienced before. I never knew that going to church could make you feel so good. I returned to the church, which was called Patton Christian Fellowship, the following Sunday, which was the fourth Sunday of November in 1992. I don't recall what bishop preached about, all I know is that it was so powerful that I could not sit in my seat. When the invitation was presented to those who desired to be saved, I walked up the aisle with my son Corey and we gave our lives to Christ along with eleven others.

In three weeks my life had been transformed. By week four, I no longer desired to go out to the club. I was no longer drinking or smoking and I had begun to start reading the Bible. The words no longer looked like Greek and I was beginning to learn about how much God loved me. The following Wednesday, we went to Bible study and Corey and I were both eager to learn. I soon learned that the voice I thought I was hearing was actually the Holy Spirit and that the reason that I had felt so dirty after my sexual encounter with Simmons was because of my previous spiritual encounter. I was taught that when God has a work for us to do, He will cause some of us to experience Him in a more personal way. I became so hungry to find out more about God and to learn His Word. I began spending hours reading and studying the Bible. My hashish buddy saw me a few days after I got saved. I did not say anything, but as soon as he saw me he asked me "did you get saved?" I asked him how he knew and he said he could see the glow. Solathian and Katecia were returning the following week and I knew Solathian would be both shocked and unprepared for the change that had taken place in me.

Psalm 145:19 "He will fulfill the desire of them that fear him: he also will hear their cry, and will save them."

A New Woman

Solathian and Katecia returned as scheduled and I was glad to see them both. I only needed Tashona back home and I would have my family back. The first day of their return, I began to tell Solathian how I no longer smoked or drank and had joined church. Of course he too did not believe it just like Shorty. It was only after he began to see for himself that he believed me. I thought that my involvement in church would make things better for us, but I soon found out that wasn't the case. Solathian was still being Solathian and the tension between us was still the same. Although I wasn't going out anymore, he still was. I didn't smoke or drink – he still did. I kept going to church because it was there that I got the peace and patience to deal with my unhappy home life. Only after I met the prophetess did I find out that the answer to my problems would be revealed through my prayers.

Additionally, Shorty and I weren't talking as much anymore. I still loved her like my sister and we were still cool, but we were in two different places in our lives. I honestly did not know how to find balance in being her friend without doing what we used to do while embracing my new life. I knew we would always be friends, but we no longer had the same things in common. Even at work, the people I worked with knew things about me had changed. I shied away from conversations I usually was in the middle of and no longer commented on other's people's business. I was no longer cursing and no longer talking about my weekends at the club. I saw everything as a sin and was becoming religious and not spiritual. I would soon find out that living a saved life did not mean I had to give up my dance. I just needed to change partners.

St. Mark 11:24 Therefore I say unto you, what things soever ye
desire, when ye pray, believe that ye receive them,
and ye shall have them."

The Prophetess

It was at Patton Christian fellowship that God introduced me to a woman who impacted my life to such a degree that I came to call her my spiritual mother and love her like a sister to this day. She is Prophetess Karan Brassfield. When new converts come into the fold, we are considered "babes" in Christ. Babes tend to choose and cling to the more mature saints in the church. In my case Karan chose me. One Sunday, I had an experience with what I came to find out later was the same Holy Spirit that I had experienced when I first began going to church, only in a different way. Although I did not scream out like Mrs. Mae Foster, I definitely believed that I felt what Mrs. Mae had felt when she would buck and shout in St. John Baptist Church. Karan came over and watched over me as I came down off that magnificent high and gave me her phone number. Although I had experimented with different drugs in my life, there was not one that could compare to the feeling of God's anointing entering a room. Karan took me under her wing and began to teach me about the Word of God. She opened up her home to me and other ladies, praying for and with us. She also taught us how to pray effectively. She taught us about fasting and how fasting and prayer go hand and hand. We were also taught that in order to have a true "relationship" with God, you had to spend time in prayer and meditation with Him. It was all so new to me and it seemed like I was moving extremely fast. But the more I learned, the more I wanted to learn. Karan taught me about "soul ties" and "generational curses." As she taught, I became more aware of why I did some of the things I did in the past, most importantly, I realized how much I needed God in my life.

The more I learned, the more I was able to apply godly principles to my life and the more I prayed for my husband and my children. Although I did not see a sudden change, as I did when I asked to be delivered from cigarettes, I knew in my heart that God was hearing my prayers – one day my husband would be saved too. It was also through Karan that I realized how real demonic spirits were. I saw people get delivered from demonic spirits with my own eyes. It was so unnerving to me to the point that I questioned if I really wanted to be a part of my new saved life. Through it all, Karan stood by me and I knew without a doubt she was one of God's anointed ones.

The more I read the Bible, the more I began to reflect on my past. The Bible proclaims that when Jesus died on the cross he took all of our sins with him and if we ask for forgiveness he would forgive us. I thought about how I had been with Corey's father, a married man and how I could have been killed while lying in his home and in their bed. I thought of all the times I had been so high or drunk until I didn't remember driving home. I thought of when I was in Kentucky and stole food to feed my children and had never gotten caught. How I lived in rough parts of town and had never gotten hurt. Through all of this, I began to realize that God had been watching over me and protecting me even when rightfully I deserved to be punished. When I would pray, so much pain was released from my heart. I began to forgive people I never thought I would forgive. I began to let go of things that I never thought I could. And I began to ask God to forgive me for the wrong things I had done. There was another area in my life that I realized that had not been addressed and that was my first sexual encounter and the molestation. Initially I did not realize the impact that either had on my life, but as I began to read more and learn more, I realized that everything that we do or that is done to us affects us in one way or another spiritually. I asked God to help me forgive those that had hurt me either intentionally or unintentionally and to cleanse my heart.

When I thought of how far God had brought me in such a short time, I remembered Karan prophesying that God had a call on my life. At the time I was not sure fully what she meant, but I knew that if God had something for me to do, I wanted to do it. It was at this time that I first realized how much God loved me. All of the time I had been looking for love in all the wrong places, the one who loved me most was watching over me and loving me with *agape* love. The bible teaches that God loves because it is His nature and the expression of His being, not because we deserve to be loved, but because it is His nature to do so, and He must be true to His nature and character. He showed this love when he allowed His son, Jesus, to die on the cross for our sins.

The morning of Father's Day I got up as usual preparing for church and getting the children ready as well. I was shocked when Solathian stated that he would be going to church with us. I thought back to how Karan and I had fasted on several occasions and prayed that Solathian would get saved. Patton was a church that was full of ministers. There were seven in particular and each of them had their own special gift. The congregation never knew who would be preaching from one Sunday to the next. On this morning when we walked in the church, I was praying that one minister in particular would be the one preaching because he was about our same age and I felt Solathian would relate more to him.

All of my praying partners and Karan gasped when in walked my little family. They were as excited as I was. When God blessed one he blessed us all because Karan taught us that God is not a "respecter of person." Just as I had prayed, Minister Childs was the one preaching. I don't remember what he preached, but when he finished and began to sing for the alter call–an invitation for those who wanted to accept Jesus as their savior–to my surprise, Solathian got up. With tears running down his face, he walked into the arms of Minister Childs' like a child walking into the arms of his mother. On Father's Day 1993, exactly six months from the time I had gotten saved, Mr. Nuniss gave his life to Christ. It was one of the best days of my life and I was thrilled to know that no matter how our situation ended up, when our lives were over on earth, we both would be with our Father in Heaven. It was nothing I had done, God did it all. All I could do as his wife was pray and let God do what he does best–bless.

Solathian joined the church and immediately began to get active by participating in Bible study and Sunday school. There weren't a lot of men in the church so there was not anyone there for him as Karan had been for me. As a result, oftentimes Solathian tagged along with the ladies when we visited other church services.

Our relationship got better because he stopped going out and drinking. As a consequence, we were left with a lot of time to have to finally deal with each other. We were definitely still trying to work things out between us. The main thing I learned during this time is that the more we were trying the more it seemed like things were going wrong. Through the struggles, Karan began to prepare me. She enlightened me to the fact that the more we got into the Word of God, the more the "enemy" (the devil) would try to make things harder for us. Marriage is one of God's greatest covenants between man and woman, therefore the devil hated our covenant. I quickly found out what she meant.

Ephesians 4:11, 12 "and he gave some apostles, and some, prophets, and some evangelists, and some, pastors and teachers. For the perfecting of the saints, for the work of the ministry, for the edifying of the body of Christ..."

Spiritual Warfare

One thing that I found out quickly from hanging out with the prophetess was that by hanging with her, I had to be prepared to see anything. I can recall several church events that we were apart of that involved someone being delivered from something. Having a Baptist background, I had no idea what was going on in the beginning. One night, we were summoned over to my neighbor's home to pray for her daughter who had become very rebellious. Her mother learned that she had been hanging with some of the German children that were into witchcraft. Myself and Karen, her husband Will, our pastors and her mother all gathered in her room and began to pray as she sat there looking bored. I recall Will telling us to close our eyes before he began praying. Well, I was hard headed and kept my eyes open looking around. I noticed the female pastor worshipping and did not think that much of it but it was not her usual worship. She was usually more reserved in her worship. Then our eyes met and I saw that the spirit was not on the child but on the female pastor! It was a mocking spirit! The spirit saw that I saw it and started walking toward me and I started screaming! Everyone was looking at me like I was crazy and all I could say was "Its on her". Needless to say, it took Karan to calm me down and it was she that believed me because a man had tried to choke her once that had a spirit on him.

My theory was proven a few weeks later at a church that we visited. It was actually a set up by God, who wanted me to get rid of the spirit of fear that I had contracted from my experience at my neighbor's house. The place was packed but somehow i got ushered up to the second row (God). The female pastor that I saw the spirit in was sitting on the front row. I looked back for Karan who was sitting at the back and she nodded to me that It was ok. At the end of the service, the speaker called the female pastor up to pray for her. As she stood before the speaker and the speaker began to pray, she began to move her body like a snake would move on the ground and after everyone in the room began to pray in tongues, the female pastor fell out under the Spirit. She was delivered and so was I. As soon as she hit the floor, I jumped up and almost knocked every chair over on my row shouting!

I saw many other things during my walk with the prophetess and received my own fair share of deliverance. I became a witness that Good will overcome evil everytime. A deliverance ministry is not for everyone and is not one that you can be apart of and play around in. Spiritual Warfare is real. If we believe in Angels we must also believe that there are demons and demonic forces. Although we should be aware, we should not be afraid because Greater is He that is in us, Than He that is in the World. Jesus defeated the devil on the Cross therefore we do not have to fear him.

I Peter 5:8 Be sober, be vigilant; because your adversary
the devil walks about like a roaring lion, seeking whom he may
devour. Resist him, steadfast in the daith, knowing that the same
sufferings are experienced by your brotherhood in the world.

Let's Separate

fter only a few months of him joining the church, things between Solathian and I began to get unbearable again. He had lost his enthusiasm for church and began to start hanging out again. This mainly came about because he was a person used to having a lot of friends. The truth of the matter was that there were not a lot of men at the church and the ones who were there did not embrace him the way that Karan and the ladies at Patton had embraced me. I realized that not having his friends around and hanging out in clubs had not been replaced by anything. I understood his position but did not know how to fix it. I soon realized I could not fix it, only God could.

Tashona was finally living with us again, so I had my entire family back. My job working in finance was going well although I sometimes felt like an outcast. Some of my co-workers began to avoid me because I talked about God so much. I don't blame them entirely because looking back in retrospect, just as with Shorty, I don't think I really knew how to handle things or people from my previous life and my changed life at the same time. I lacked balance in my relationships with others as well as in my family life.

The interactions between Solathian and I got to the point of non-existent. We were living in the same house but we were hardly speaking to one another. I was confused and hurt and still trying to pray, but I really wanted to get mad and cuss him out. Something inside of me would not allow me. I prayed more and more. The more I prayed, the worse things got. Then one day Solathian told me he was moving out and into the barracks. I was so hurt. I could not understand how we had come so far in God to fall so far apart from each other.

I leaned on Karan and the other ladies from the church for prayer. I was having a hard time understanding but every day, Karan would call and encourage me. She would fast with me and more than anything, she would listen to me. She never allowed me to feel sorry for myself. She would always ask, "What does the Word say?" If it wasn't lined up with what the Word of God said, she told me it was a lie. I began to pray more for myself and the situation. Solathian moved out December 1993, six months after he had gotten saved and right when I got the news.

Psalm 55:17 "Evening, and morning, and at noon, will I pray, and cry aloud: and he shall hear my voice."

The Prophecy

$\mathscr{P}$atton Christian Fellowship had under gone some changes over the year. We had a new pastor, as the Bishop had returned to the states. The new pastor was a wonderful pastor as well. I had become an usher and one particular Sunday as I was standing in the back of the church ushering, the pastor's wife began to pray and prophesy. She prophesied of a woman in the congregation whose womb had been closed for many years that God was now opening. She continued on and as I listened such a feeling of grief came over me and all I remember was feeling light headed and I apparently passed out.

When I came to, I had been taken to an area in the foyer and there were other ministers praying for me. I remember thinking, the pastor's wife was praying about me. It had been almost three years since I had had the abortion and I had not been on any birth control since. I had not thought about any of it before that moment in a long time and when I went home I cried and prayed and asked God to forgive me once again for killing my child. It was different this time when I prayed. This time I felt in my spirit that God had forgiven me and that now I had to learn to forgive myself.

In spite of our tumultuous relationship, Solathian and I would see each other intimately every now and then, but after a while we stopped. Although he was *my* husband, I knew he was seeing other women. I could not stand that thought, yet it was out of my control. It was about three months after the prophecy that I began not feeling well so I made an appointment to go to the doctor. I wasn't feeling much better after he gave me the diagnosis, after three years of not being on birth control, I was all of a sudden pregnant!

Job 29:3 "My glory was fresh in me,
and my bow was renewed in my hand."

You Shall Have A Son

I had mixed emotions about being pregnant again. I was happy because I felt God had given me another chance to make things right, but on the other hand I looked at the fact that my husband and I were separated and I had three other children. By this time I was twenty-nine years old.

Solathian was temporarily in the States for school when I learned I was pregnant. When he returned I told him but he did not believe me. It was only when he saw my enlarged belly that he believed it. No, he did not move back in and we lived happily ever after, far from it. He stayed in the barracks and was having the time of his life. I would see him sometimes riding with his friends and would get so angry. Here I was, walking around with his child in my belly and he was out doing whatever. I cried and prayed all the time. Sometimes I was angry and sometimes I wasn't. If it had not been for praying and my church family, I know I would have lost my resolve. So many times I wanted to walk away from living saved and return to what I was doing before, but something inside me would not allow me. I knew I had to hold on.

I remember praying one night and God spoke to me. Not audibly, but to my spirit. He told me I was having a son and to name him Jeremiah. God also told me to breastfeed him and to pray Jeremiah 1:4-5 over my belly and I did. Solathian's mother called one day and I told her the news of my pregnancy. I could tell in her voice that she was not pleased. Although I was not surprised, she asked me if I thought it would be a good idea for me to have another child considering that Solathian was planning to divorce me. It was just like before except this time I was in another place spiritually. I let her know in a respectful manner that it did not matter what he did because God would make a way for me and my children. With that being said, I got off the phone and prayed some more.

I was still working every day. I had gained so much weight that it was becoming more and more difficult to get around. I knew that I would have to eventually quit, although technically I could not afford to. Karan kept telling me, "The Lord will take care of you if you trust him." After hearing that and reading all of the acts of faith in the bible, I began to pray for God to increase my faith to the point that no matter what situations looked like, I would continue to trust him. I left my job at the Department of Defense in July trusting that God would supply for all of my needs like the bible said. I admit, there were times I questioned if leaving the job was the right thing to do but God always came through for me. The more God blessed me with peace of mind, finances, or strength to get out of bed another day, the more my faith increased.

The pregnancy was a long nine months and I did a lot of crying. Thus, it was no surprise when Jeremiah finally arrived on September 14, 1994 that he was a weeping prophet just like Jeremiah in the Bible. I had a few complications with the delivery and the doctors had to induce my labor but Karan and some others were there praying for me. It was weird but a spirit of fear had come over me during labor. I had given birth to three children already, but it was as if I was having my first baby. Needless to say, the fear drove my blood pressure up and that is why my labor had to be induced. I was surprised but Solathian was actually there. He stayed with me the entire time and even went into the delivery room with me. I don't know what happened but when he cut the umbilical cord, the Holy Spirit came over him and he began to jump up and down. Something spiritual definitely took place and only he and God knows what it was. Solathian wanted me to make the baby a junior because they looked so much like one another, but I told him what God had said. His last words before leaving the hospital were "he looks like a junior."

That night I prayed and I asked the Lord to put Solathian and me on one accord if He had truly told me to name my child Jeremiah. The next day when he came to the hospital he told me if God said name the baby Jeremiah, then the name should be Jeremiah. I was utterly thrilled with the confirmation from God. I went home the next day but after a rough night of unsuccessfully trying to breastfeed Jeremiah (the way God had instructed me) and my feet swelling to the size of small balloons, I knew I was going to have to go back to the hospital. Jeremiah and I cried the entire night while Solathian and the children lay all around us snoring. After returning to the hospital the next day, they ended up keeping me. I had continued complications from preeclampsia, which is a pregnancy condition caused by high blood pressure and having protein in the urine. I remained in the hospital for a week after Jeremiah was born due to the complications from the high blood pressure. As a result, Jeremiah and the other children stayed with Karan and her family. At the time Karan had all girls and had always wanted a son, therefore she and her husband Will became Jeremiah's god-parents. I found myself with a new baby and hopes of reconciliation with my husband. If only someone had given Solathian the memo.

Jeremiah 1:5 "Before I formed thee in the belly I knew thee, and before thou calmest forth out of the womb I sanctified thee, and I ordained thee a prophet unto the nations."

Headed Back South

Prior to going into the hospital, I was beginning to realize that things between Solathian and I simply were not working out. However, I held on and refused to believe it, mainly because of the last prophecy I had received. While pregnant, I had visited a church with Karan and some other ladies when a lady came to me, introduced herself and began to prophesy. She prophesied, "You and your husband are going to get back together and it is going to better than it ever was before." The last prophecy I had received had been so accurate that I wanted this one to also be true.

During the months that followed, everything seemed to be going contrary to the prophecy. I had a flashback to how Solathian and I initially got together. I had been married and cheated on my first husband, Brandon, and now all of the things I had done to him were being done to me. When I flashed back further I remembered the time spent with Corey's father while he was married. Oh yes! Payday had finally come full force. It didn't take me long to realize that the seeds I had sown years prior were no longer seeds–they were weeds.

I finally began to understand that the only way that Solathian and I would be together was if the Lord did it. I sought the Lord and felt that my time in Germany was coming to an end. I prayed about it constantly and when I finally felt peace about it, I began preparing for the move. I called for housing to pick up the furniture and for the car to be shipped. Additionally, I got assistance from Solathian's commander in getting orders for tickets to fly home to Arkansas. I don't know why Solathian would not help me get what I needed to go home but when I told him I was leaving, he let me know that he was not going to help me leave. I don't know if he was being mean, if he just liked the idea of having his cake and eating it too or if he really did not want to lose his family. Regardless the reason, as a civilian, I had military contacts that helped me get everything that I needed to return to the United States. My friends Shorty and Debra had been long gone and now my turn had come.

With a newborn, I had to wait until Jeremiah turned one month old before the Army would let us fly. I had a long eight hour flight ahead and my four children were aged thirteen, eleven, five and 1 month. I wasn't looking forward to it, but I knew it had to be done. I had good children so I did not foresee any problems.

Prior to me leaving I had begun attending Pastor Fitzgerald's church. Pastor Fitzgerald was once a member of Patton and was active duty military. He had started a Bible study that eventually led him to starting a church. We called our sanctuary "The Upper Room" because it was located upstairs (maid quarters) in the military housing unit that Karan and Will lived. Pastor Fitzgerald was an awesome teacher and pastor, he was Caucasian and did not feel the least bit intimidated by the fact that he was the only Caucasian in the bunch. He was down to earth and everybody loved him. I began working with the youth ministry at his church. It started out as just a way to help the ministry but I quickly fell in love with working with the children and seeing them grow in the Lord. I understood that training up a child to know God at a young age was truly essential to their future just as the bible speaks of in Proverbs 22:6. I further believed that teaching them to have a personal relationship with God should be a major part of that training. That was the component that I had lacked as a child.

By the time Jeremiah was to be christened, the church had moved into an actual church building. The membership was still small but size did not matter, we had a Pastor that enlightened us every Sunday with God's Word. This would be our last Sunday before heading home so after the christening, Pastor Fitzgerald awarded me with a plaque for working with the youth ministry and also gave me an envelope that I later found had $1,000.00 cash in it. That may not sound like a lot of money, but to someone that had $0, it was a lot. I was truly grateful because I had no idea what I was going to do until I would be able to get unemployment or a job. I will never forget what they did for me and I know God in return has blessed them accordingly.

The following week, Katecia, Corey, Tashona, Jeremiah and I got in the car with Karan and Will and headed to the airport in Frankfurt Germany on our way back South. I did not see Solathian that day. I figured it was probably best. But as we headed toward that airport and I looked at my children, a sense of peace came over me and I knew that we would be okay. Solathian would be okay. He had God in his heart and I knew that one day God was going to draw him back with his staff the way that a good shepherd does. I felt that I had forgiven him for his part in the demise of our marriage and I tried to forgive myself knowing that he was not totally at fault. We had been young and immature but I felt the story was still not over and that God had not revealed the big picture of why he paired the two of us together. My heart was hurting because I was still in love with my husband, but I knew what I was doing was the right thing. It takes courage and faith to leave something that you love but I had to believe that God had not brought us that far to leave us. Only time would tell if I had truly forgiven him, if it was indeed the end of the story and how awesome God would work in both of our lives.

After a teary goodbye and lots of hugs from Karan and Will, we boarded the plane. Over the years, I would miss Karan and my spiritual family in Germany, but I hold dear to what Karan told me before I left. She said, "God has allowed you to grow up fast in him and you are going to be fine as long as you continue to pray and trust Him, he has a work for you to do."

As I lay my head back on my seat and prepared for the long flight, I looked out the window trying to see Karan leaving the airport parking lot. I almost felt like grabbing the children and running off the plane. For a brief moment, I became fearful and felt totally lost. I was about to start my life all over again with four children, no job and no place to stay that I could call my own. Before the thoughts could overtake me, I began to think of how God had shown his love toward me by first revealing my issues to me and then by giving me His solutions to those issues through His Word (the bible). God had used Pastor Fitzgerald and my church family to show me and my family love by blessing us monetarily. I also thought of the Bishop and Pastor Boswell who showed my family love at the church by teaching us the Word of God. But most of all I thought about all those years I had been *looking for love in all the wrong places.* I looked for it in people, in things, in alcohol and in drugs. I did not realize that in order to experience true love I had to first love myself and see myself the way God saw me. I had to also respect my mind and my body enough to know that I was beautifully and wonderfully made and that no man should have been allowed to lower my self-esteem or take away my precious virginity. God created my mother and father and they were the vehicles that he used to transport me to earth. Though they were not married when I was conceived, I was still a blessing. I look how I look because God himself formed me in my mother's womb. I came to realize that the void that I had been trying so hard to fill was reserved for God and nothing else had the power to fill it. It was when I began to love "my temple" that my life had begun to change internally in preparation for eternity.

Were things in my life perfect now? No. Were things hard at times? Yes. Did I want to give up, almost give up, or gave up if only for a moment? Yes. But one thing I did not do is stop believing in the power of God.

Now I was on my way back to Arkansas, there were definitely some fences that God needed to mend there. Over the years things between my mother and I had gotten much better though I felt there was still room for improvement on both of our parts. I was up for the challenge because I knew that the battle was not mine–it was the Lord's. I rested in the fact that I had gained some powerful insight. I now knew that when there is a man in my life, God loves me when there is not a man in my life. God loves me. When friends or family leave or forsake me, God says he will not do either. When I have money, God loves me. When I don't have money, God still loves me. I know He will never cheat and I know I can call Him day or night and He will be there. I don't have to smoke weed to experience Him and I don't have to drink to keep Him. I know now that all the love I could ever need or want is in HIM. There is nothing that I can do to earn it because He gives his love freely, with no strings attached. I can call on Him early in the morning or in the midnight hour and he won't push the "ignore" button. If I did not have legs–I would still be able to stand in God. In spite of my weaknesses and flaws, *God's Love* has proven to be unconditional!

I wish I could say that when I arrived down South everything was perfect and I never made another mistake. I wish I could say that I was so saved and Holy Ghost filled that I had it all together. NOT. What I did have, however, was power and love for myself. I knew that I no longer had to compromise my self-worth to get love from another individual and did not have to use drugs or sex to numb how I felt about myself. God created me to be me and no one could be me better than I could. Low self-esteem had been my enemy and when I got saved, God gave me the power through prayer to fight the enemy.

They say "what don't kill you will make you stronger." Trust me when I say, when I arrived back in Arkansas, everything God placed inside of me was soon put to the test...

II Corinthians 5:17 "Therefore if any man be in Christ,
he is a new creature: old things are passed away,
behold all things are become new."

Prayer of Salvation:

Father God, in the name of Jesus, I acknowledge that I am a sinner. I ask that you forgive me for my sins both knowingly and unknowingly and cleanse me from all unrighteousness. I believe that you lived and died for my sins and after 3 days you rose from the grave with all power in your hands and now sit at the right hand of the Father. I further believe that salvation is a gift and that there is nothing that I can do to earn it, but it is given freely by you. I confess that you are Lord of Lords and King of Kings and I accept this gift of salvation. Help me to commit to serving you with my whole heart. In Jesus' name I pray. Amen.

My Prayer for you:

Father God, I thank you and I praise you for the opportunity to be able to write this book. I pray that everyone that reads this book will be blessed. I pray for their families, their situations, and their circumstances. I pray against every hindering spirit that would try to keep them bound. I plead the blood of Jesus against every demonic spirit and force that would try and keep them from walking in his or her wealthy place which is their destiny. I thank you that no weapon formed against them shall be able to prosper and every tongue that rises against them in judgment shall be condemned. I thank you that it is done according to your Word. In Jesus' name I pray. Amen.

James 5:16 "Confess your faults one to another, that ye may be healed. The effectual fervent prayer of a righteous man availeth much."

About The Author

*T*wana Nuniss lives in Little Rock, Arkansas. She is the mother of four children: Corey, Tashona, Katecia and Jeremiah. This is her first book – a story of storms, deceit, pain and triumphs.

In regards to writing *Looking for Love,* Twana states, "The Lord put this book in my spirit in 2003 and I have worked on it over the years. It was initially a personal journal. My intent was not to embarrass my family or make anyone uncomfortable. My intent was to expose the enemy that was in me. For years I was held captive by my past and I could not move forward in the things of God because I was still carrying baggage, secrets, hurts and pain. God wanted me to get free so the enemy would not have anything on me. This is the avenue that He chose for me to get my deliverance and to help others get free in the process."

Twana is Principal Broker of Nuniss Realty in Little Rock, Arkansas and founder of "The Last shall be First Mentoring Program" and God's Way Publishing LLC.

Made in the
USA
Columbia, SC